THE STORY OF UNITY CHURCH
1872-1972
Revised Edition
by
Elinor Sommers Otto

Reredos Press
St. Paul, Minnesota

The Story of Unity Church, 1872-1972
Revised Edition
by Elinor Sommers Otto
© COPYRIGHT 1972, 2020 Unity Church of St. Paul
ISBN: 978-1-950996-02-5

Reredos Press
A Program of Unity Church-Unitarian
732 Holly Ave
St. Paul, MN 55104

It is for us to bear in our hearts...the concerted good of the past that we may feel the strength of the heritage and be thankful, but dedicate ourselves to the future — a future of active religion together.

—Wallace W. Robbins

Acknowledgments

This book is the result of a tentative suggestion made by Arthur Foote that "someone should write a history of Unity Church." To the late Harry G. Huse we owe the original compilation and writing of a briefer chronicle, concluding with Frederick May Eliot's term of ministry, from which this expanded, and more detailed account has been developed.

We are indebted to Elwood Maunder, a former St. Paulite and member of Unity Church, who, in 1960-61, gathered from the corners of the church building much of the historical material now filed at the Minnesota Historical Society.

Acknowledgments are especially due to the following persons who searched their memories for data and anecdotes: Walter L. Chapin, Jr., Mary Davis, Josephine Downey, Mary Chapin Heisig, Martha Putnam Holman, Elizabeth Ames Jackson, Eleanor Jilson, Wallace W. Robbins, Helen James Sommers, Esther Tiffany, and William L. West, Jr. Many others have contributed information. Gertrude Sheadle Hatch and Elizabeth M. Whitman have answered countless questions. I owe special thanks to Helen Thane Katz for her patient instruction, guidance, and criticism in the editing and revising of the manuscript and to Arthur N. Foote for providing details, for rewording passages, and for giving me the benefit of his fund of knowledge about the church, its members, and the denomination. The staff of the Minnesota Historical Society was of valuable assistance in searching out material. Alan Seaburg, now curator of manuscripts at the Andover-Harvard Theological Library, has been generous with his help and encouragement. In addition, I wish to express my appreciation to Jean Vosberg West who so competently undertook the business detail involved in producing this book.

Finally, for omitting names of those loyal members who also played significant roles in the history of our church, I apologize, since it is impossible, within the space allotted, to include all those who have contributed to the progress and welfare of our Unitarian society in St. Paul.

—Elinor Sommers Otto, St. Paul, September 15, 1971

Introduction to the Revised Edition

I've often wondered if Ellie Otto knew just how valuable her history of Unity Church would turn out to be. It's 50 years since she worked on the project, and it is so important to us that we feel the need to reprint the book and make it available again to Unity members and friends.

This revised edition contains additional photographs and has a different format, but we have preserved the original language, organization, information, and footnotes (for the most part).

We are all indebted to Elinor Sommers Otto and all who worked on the history of our first 100 years. She lived all of her 90 years in St. Paul. When she died in 2003, Unity Church lost a beloved member but she will long be remembered for, among many things, the enormous task of making our history accessible and real to all present and future members of Unity Church-Unitarian.

Last but not least, thank you to all the archivists of Unity Church, past and present. Your work is greatly appreciated.
  —Shelley Butler, Editor, Revised Edition, February 24, 2020

Ministers and Ministerial Staff of Unity Church and the Years That They Served

1872-1876		John R. Effinger
1877-1883		William Channing Gannett
1884-1886		Clay MacCauley
1886-1894		Samuel McChord Crothers
1895-1897		William R. Lord
1898-1900		Clarence L. Diven
1900-1907		Richard W. Boynton
1908-1917		John Dumont Reid
1917-1937		Frederick May Eliot
1938-1944		Wallace W. Robbins
1945-1970		Arthur N. Foote; Minister Emeritus, 1970-
	1948-1972	Elizabeth M. Whitman; Director of Religious Education
	1955-1959	Ronald J. Walrath; Assistant Minister
	1963-1964	Lon Ray Call; Interim Minister
	1966-1970	Frederick A. Rutledge; Associate Minister
1971- 1999		Roy D. Phillips
2001-2021		Janne and Rob Eller-Isaacs

Table of Contents

Illustrations

I. Foundations 1852-1872

There were Unitarians in St. Paul long before there was a Unitarian church, or the prospect of one. Unlike some of the early Minnesota settlers of other denominations, the Unitarians were not missionaries seeking to convert the Indians or bring back to a state of grace the hard-living American frontiersmen. They were not members of a religious movement, nor had they traveled west as a pioneering group. They were, it seems, just hardy, adventurous people, impelled for a variety of reasons to leave their homes and establish themselves in a promising new territory.

Although many of these early Unitarians appear to have come from New England, there is no evidence that the various persons had known one another before leaving. Despite their liberal beliefs they were not fleeing persecution. In fact, there already existed in Boston a certain forbearance for those dissenters, some of them quite prominent, who could not accept the gospel of the Trinity. This was more tolerance than they were to encounter in St. Paul for some time.

No matter where these migrants had originated, they seem to have been individuals of strong beliefs (or disbeliefs, according to one's viewpoint), and they brought their Unitarian convictions with them. Eventually they became acquainted in their new environment and acquired a loose bond of mutual interest. By 1852 some recognition of their existence must have occurred elsewhere in Unitarian circles. In June of that year the Reverend George Woodward of Galena, Illinois, journeyed up the Mississippi River to St. Paul and held a single service for Unitarians in a hall rented from the Sons of Temperance. We do not know how many people attended that service nor who they were.

That single sermon had to suffice, however, for the next six years. The Unitarians in the settlement were too few and their means too meager to finance renting halls for additional meetings. St. Paul, after a burst of expansion and speculation during which it earned the reputation of being "the fastest and liveliest town on the Mississippi" had been thrown into turmoil, as was the rest of the United States, by the great financial panic of 1857. From Mrs. Newell, wife of the Reverend Frederick R. Newell, of whom more later, we have this comment on the plight of the St. Paulites: "Everybody was poor—oh, so poor were some that one of them who had lived in luxury was driven to ask at the shops for the meat that had been put aside to be sold for dog's meat!"[1]

It was in 1858, when recovery from the '57 panic was slowly getting under way, that Frederick R. Newell, an inactive Unitarian minister from Boston, traveled up the Mississippi as a passenger on a sternwheeler. He came not as a minister but as a settler intent upon establishing himself in some business that would support him and his wife. That enterprise was to be a feed store on Robert Street.

The newcomers were welcomed by the Unitarians in St. Paul and, when Newell's former vocation became known, his services as a minister were earnestly solicited by Benjamin Drew, speaking for the group. Newell, finding that launching his business was taking all his time and energy, explained that he would have no opportunity to prepare new sermons. But since he did have a collection of old ones in his trunk he agreed, if those would be acceptable, to lead a congregation and preach regularly every Sunday, providing a meeting place could be furnished. His offer was gratefully accepted. The first such sermon was presented December 12, 1858, in a hall over Pollock and Donaldson Company's store on Robert Street. It had been preceded by a small notice Drew inserted in the St. Paul *Daily Minnesotian* announcing the time and place and inviting the public to attend. Thirty-four people, seven of them children, listened to Newell preach on the subject of "worship."

---

[1] William H. Kelley Journal, Minnesota Historical Society, 160. Mrs. Frederick Newell to Mrs. Charles Clark, February 24, 1892, in Kelley journal. An invaluable record of this era is the journal of William H. Kelley, which begins with the events of 1858. This church chronicle was maintained by Kelley until his death in 1900, and thereafter until 1928 by his daughter Emma and others.

Figure 1 Reverend Frederick R. Newell
Minnesota Historical Society

Frederick Newell's supply of old sermons and the devotion he
displayed, despite the demands of his business, carried the
regular Sunday services for almost ten months, until the
second Sunday in October, 1859. From the first meeting place
the services had been moved to the Philharmonic Society
quarters in the old Concert Hall Building on the bluff side of

what was then Third Street. On the side facing the river the building contained five stories, the lower two being below the street level. The Concert Hall, located on the second floor, was one floor immediately below the sidewalk. This led a visiting minister of this period—the Reverend James Freeman Clark—to carry back to Boston the report that he had preached to the Unitarians of St. Paul "in a cellar."

The "cellar" was falling into disrepair and could be rented cheaply. But in June of 1859 it became unavailable, and the meetings had to be moved to the Good Templars' Hall on the corner of Fifth and Robert.

Only a few statistics of that first ten months of Unitarian activities can be gleaned from the old records. The average Sunday attendance was around thirty persons. Once, when a visiting minister came up the Mississippi to preach a Sunday sermon, the number crept up to forty. The financial picture of the church during the ten months was simple and explicit:

Rent, including sexton's compensation	$70.30
Printing	$1.00
Minister's compensation	$21.00
Total	$92.30

Included in the brief statement of finances was a list of the sixteen people who contributed to sustain the earliest organization. Among those named were William H. Kelley, Charles E. Mayo, Joseph S. Sewall, Charles H. Clark, John DeGraw, Benjamin Drew, Louis E. Fisher, and Charles Creek.

Modest as the budget was, averaging $9.23 per month, it was more, apparently, than the little group could afford. The records state only that this first effort toward a Unitarian church was discontinued "from pecuniary circumstances" (as

4

Figure 2 Mr. and Mrs. William Kelley

William Henry Kelley of St. Paul, 1858. Minnesota Historical Society

Henrietta Maria Hancock Kelley (Mrs. William Henry Kelley) of St. Paul, 1858. Minnesota Historical Society

William Channing Gannett, the second minister of Unity Church, expressed it in his chronicle, "The Story of Our Church").[2] For a few haphazard weeks, small meetings were held at the homes of members but shortly that activity also was abandoned.

Newell continued his feed business for a while longer and then, with the outbreak of the Civil War, joined the Union Army as a chaplain. Two members of his congregation left these tributes to his short pastorate:

---

[2] Kelley Journal, 8. Interpolated with Kelley's account is the brief history of Unity Church by William Channing Gannett, "The Story of Our Church." It was originally delivered as a sermon on March 2, 1879, and copied into the journal from the original.

(From an unidentified lady member), "Mr. Newell was a brave, good man and did his very best to found a church here, but the time was not ripe."[3]

(From Benjamin Drew, already mentioned), "Mr. Newell labored earnestly and faithfully and acceptably to disseminate the doctrines he loved so well and of which he was a shining exemplar.... He died, as he had always lived, in the line of duty—a chaplain encouraging the hands and hearts of Union soldiers in the war of the Rebellion."[4]

It is interesting to take a brief look at the St. Paul of 1858-59, when these efforts at keeping Unitarianism alive were taking place. At the beginning of '58 Minnesota was still a territory, with a claimed population of 150,000. In May it was admitted to the Union. St. Paul had a population variously given as between 6,500 and 10,000. Two railroads had reached the Mississippi from the East, but the nearest terminal was at La Crosse. Passenger and freight traffic still had to come up the Mississippi by steamboat, and Red River carts were trundling their way across the prairies to the west. The ferry crossing the river was presently to be replaced by a bridge. This ferry and its environs could be clearly seen from the "cellar" where the early Unitarian services were held. The unknown woman whose tribute to Newell has been quoted mentions that looking out the southern window "we could also see the Indian village built of teepees [sic] which every winter appeared on the opposite flats, and the burial places of the Indians which in winter were in trees in which the corpse, well wrapped up and provided with provisions for the dark journey and, if a brave, with arms to defend himself, was laid. In the spring the bodies were taken to the high hill at Mendota and buried."

Regular Catholic services had been held in St. Paul since November 1841, Presbyterian and Methodist services since

---

[3] Undated and unsigned speech, Unity Church (Saint Paul, Minn.). Unity Church records. Minnesota Historical Society.
[4] Kelley Journal, 5. Benjamin Drew to William Kelley, March 7, 1879.

August 1849. Cognizance had been taken by the orthodox of the presence of a few Unitarians and their attempts to organize. In later years, Mrs. Peter Long recalled that in 1858, when she was a young girl, her father, the minister of the first Swedish church of St. Paul, "called his children together and offered family prayer in behalf of those misguided unbelievers who were meeting that morning over Pollock and Donaldson's store."[5]

Six years of the disruptions of the Civil War elapsed before St. Paul Unitarians could once more give thought to reviving their struggling group. And only once during those years had they enjoyed a Sunday service. That was on August 4, 1861, when a congregation of twelve men, six women, and thirteen children gathered in the courthouse to hear a sermon preached by the Reverend Thomas Vickers of Cincinnati, who happened to be in St. Paul. In a letter to Kelley, dated October 17, 1880, Mrs. John DeGraw recalls an interesting, if slightly distraught, account of that meeting.

The courtroom had been in use all week and was in filthy condition. Three of the women, in their working dresses, with towels and dusters, tackled it early Sunday morning and had it fairly clean by the time they changed back into their Sunday clothes for the preaching. The services proceeded as usual until it was time for the Bible reading. Unfortunately, there was no Bible. Services were halted while a search was made of a stack of volumes in one corner of the room. All turned out to be old law books except one—a copy of Byron's poems. Vickers announced another hymn and while it was being sung two gentlemen of the congregation went to the jail, interrupted a cribbage game between the jailer and his deputy, and, in a hurried joint search, discovered a Bible and rushed it back to the courtroom. The meeting, according to our narrator, continued properly, but the congregation did not escape a scolding because the Bible had been forgotten.

---

[5] Kelley Journal, 6.

Of the period immediately following the Civil War William Channing Gannett had this to say in his chronicle of the church:

> The war ended. It had done much to liberalize the religious sentiment of the country. Men who had stood on battle fields side-by-side—and women who had scraped lint or packed Sanitary Commission boxes side-by-side for four years had learnt to think less of the church fences that kept them apart in the prospering days of peace. But the Unitarian Association in the East probably thought the war had levelled these fences more than it really had: now was their golden opportunity, they thought; men now wanted the Liberal Gospel and would welcome it, and southward and westward went their missionaries![6]

During the summer of 1865 several of these missionaries came to St. Paul. The first was the Reverend H. P. Cutting from Winona. On May 28 of that year, he preached in the courtroom at the courthouse, presumably now equipped with a Bible. He was followed on July 2 by the Reverend J. Augier of Boston, who drew an audience of forty-eight persons, the largest number to date to attend a St. Paul Unitarian meeting.

Augier was an organizer as well as a preacher and he remained in St. Paul long enough to hold a meeting at the home of William L. Ames,[7] near the head of Cedar Street, to initiate plans for a Unitarian society. In the list of those St. Paulites present we again encounter familiar names: Mr. and Mrs. William L. Ames, Henry Acker, John DeGraw, Joseph Sewall, A. H. Wimbish, Channing Seabury, Mrs. H. W. Haynes, Miss Mary Sewall, and William H. Kelley.

The group christened itself the First Unitarian Society of St. Paul and correspondence was begun with the American Unitarian Association in Boston to ascertain whether a pastor could be secured. In September another missionary, the

---

[6] Kelley Journal, 10.

[7] William L. Ames was not related to the Charles Wilberforce Ames family.

Reverend William G. Scandlin, came west and preached for two successive Sundays. Throughout the following winter correspondence with the East continued and as spring neared word came from the Association that a man was available. But somehow there had been a change of heart in St. Paul. Whether the old bugaboo, "pecuniary circumstances," was again a threat is not a matter of record. We have only the account of a meeting held on March 1, 1866, at William Kelley's house on Aurora Avenue, at which Channing Seabury offered the following resolution, which was carried:

> Resolved that we deem it expedient to postpone for the present any further experiment towards establishing Unitarian preaching in St. Paul, feeling as we do that we would now labor under difficulties which at a future date would be obviated.[8]

Nearly a year passed before the Unitarians were offered another opportunity to hear a minister. That occasion was on June 3, when a fourth missionary, the Reverend William P. Tilden, found his way into St. Paul and preached a single sermon.

Circumstances were developing, however, that would give some of the St. Paul Unitarians a chance to hear liberal preaching. Until now the group, whether they called themselves Unitarians or Universalists, had joined their small forces to meet together. In August of 1865, however, those who preferred the designation "Universalist" decided to branch out on their own and hold meetings in Armory Hall. They incorporated on January 30, 1866. A resolution and terms of a proposed union between the two liberal sects were presented to the Unitarians by the new organization, but the offer was summarily rejected. No specific reason was given, but of this episode, Gannett, in his delightful manner, says, "I know not why the invitation was declined, save, perhaps, for the general reason that even when the bread is the bread of life, a man likes his own loaf best and the whole of it."[9]

---

[8] Kelley Journal, 11.
[9] Kelley Journal, 16.

From this modest start the Universalist Church, under the leadership of its minister, Herman Bisbee, had managed to keep going. After the meeting on March 1, when the Unitarians were forced to disband, those of the group who sincerely longed to have Sunday services and were sufficiently liberal to go to a church that did not bear exactly the same name as their own started attending the Universalist Church and put their energies into building it up.

Presently the Universalists purchased a lot on Wabasha and Ninth Streets where they planned to erect their church. Construction was begun in October 1867, but the building was not completed until 1872.

Sometime in 1867 Bisbee resigned from his pastorate, to be succeeded by a series of short-term preachers. Then trouble developed, with a sharp cleavage between the conservative members and the liberals over a proposed permanent minister, Daniel M. Reed, who had delivered a number of sermons during the series of short pastorates. The drastic outcome was eventually to leave the new Universalist Church building vacant; we can supply nothing more illuminating than this quote from Gannett's later charitable account of the squabble, which had taken place well before his time:

> Mr. Reed's liberality proved the wedge which split the congregation. When, in the summer of 1871 it became a question whether he should be invited to settle down with them the old divisive names Unitarian and Universalist had to spring up again. Therefore, they who had put most money into the church building being earnest and sincere conservatives, felt themselves obliged to veto the preference of what, I have understood, was the majority. Doubtless they could not have done otherwise and been loyal to their highest convictions of right and truth. But the same feeling moved those who wanted a distinctly Liberal preacher, and the consequence was one of those sad, yet almost necessary tragedies that happen in church life. Mr. Reed went away and the two parties in the church went

asunder and, for a while, I believe, there were again no Liberal services in St. Paul.[10]

One thing may be said about dissension, deplorable as it is when it strikes. Often it serves as a catalyst to precipitate definite, positive action where previously there had been hesitation.

This disagreement served to arouse the Unitarians of St. Paul and to bring them to the conclusion that they were now strong enough in numbers and resolution to make another attempt at organizing a church of their own. On October 27, 1871, at a meeting in the home of William Kelley, the sum of $1,305 was subscribed toward sustaining Unitarian preaching for one year. On December 28, 1871, with the arrival of S. S. Hunting, western secretary of the Unitarian Association, a second meeting was held, this time at the home of John D. Ludden, and those present "organized themselves into a little church—authorizing Mr. Hunting to send them at least a three months' minister."[11]

Upon adoption of the following agreement, later to be incorporated into the articles of association as a preamble, the Unitarian church in St. Paul became a reality:

> Recognizing the Fatherhood of God and the Brotherhood of Mankind, receiving Jesus as Teacher, and seeking the Spirit of Truth as the guide of our lives, in the hope of immortal life, we, the undersigned, associate ourselves to maintain the public worship of God, and promote the welfare of humanity.[12]

---

[10] Kelley Journal, 18.
[11] Kelley Journal, 19.
[12] Kelley Journal, 19. Attributed to William Channing Gannett.

11

II. Gannett and a Church Home 1872-1883

Early in 1872 the new minister selected by Hunting arrived in St. Paul. He was the Reverend John R. Effinger, whose dedicated spirit helped make possible the establishment of the St. Paul church.

Effinger had already served several Unitarian parishes. He had actually begun his ministerial career as an itinerant Methodist minister in the mountains of his native Virginia, where he was born in 1835. Then, until the end of the Civil War, he filled pulpits in Baltimore and in Washington, D. C. By that time, however, he found that his religious thought was more in harmony with Unitarianism than with his own church, and he accepted calls to parishes in Chicago and in Keokuk, Iowa.

Effinger became a substantial missionary figure in the Unitarian movement. In addition to becoming the first actual minister of Unity Church, he established other churches, including those in Des Moines, Iowa, and Bloomington, Illinois, where he served for six years. He is also remembered as one of the organizers of the Iowa Unitarian Association in Des Moines. Because of impaired health he retired from active ministerial duty at the age of forty-one. He went on to be secretary of the Iowa Unitarian Association and later of the Western Unitarian Conference and remained on this board until his death in 1902.

Effinger's first Sunday service was held February 11, 1872, in Knauft's Hall on the third floor of a building at Seventh and Olive Streets. Two weeks later, on February 25, 1872 (now considered the birth date of Unity Church), ten articles of association, signed by some fifty persons, were added to the preamble, and the following Board of Trustees was selected: W. L. Ames, Joseph S. Sewall, William H. Kelley, Daniel McCaine, Edward Sawyer, and H. P. Grant. Three of these names, it is interesting to note, had appeared on the first list of organization-minded Unitarians back in 1865. And to the list of subscribers were added other names of families now well-known to Unity Church, among them George Chapin, C. C.

Figure 3 John R. Effinger
Minister of Unity Church, 1872-1876
Minnesota Historical Society

DeCoster, David Ramaley, Charles Furness, James Boyden,
Mrs. F. G. Gersting, Abraham Bailey, Samuel J. Beals, J. F.
Blodgett.

By fall the new church was thriving sufficiently to consider
acquiring more adequate quarters than its third-floor hall. Not

only were two services being held each Sunday, one at 10:30 a.m. and another at 7:30 p.m., but a Sunday school with eleven pupils attending opened, and the enrollment soon increased to fifty-six. James Beals became superintendent and W. H. Kelley held the combined functions of secretary, treasurer, and librarian. To this information temperance-minded Kelley added, "A communion service was purchased by subscription and the first and only occasion on which it was used, the communicants partook of water."[13]

Fortunately, a small wooden church on Temperance Street, between Eighth and Ninth, became available when the growing Plymouth Church moved into larger quarters. The building could hold two hundred people. Its seats were hard and its interior was a dirty, depressing brown. Its rental was considerably more than that of Knauft's Hall and would badly exceed the budget. Once again monetary problems were plaguing the church group. But there was hope that some financial support might come from the American Unitarian Association, and the women of the church had been doing their part with "earnest Oyster Suppers, Public Balls and Opera House Dramatics," all helpfully patronized by the public.[14] There was a great deal of discussion as to the advisability of the move, but finally the courageous outvoted the timid and November 17 saw the Unitarians snugly established on Temperance Street. The hoped-for support from the East failed to materialize but the women had managed to raise the remarkable sum of $700 and the year closed with a debt of only $200.

Early in 1873 the Unitarians were saddened by the death of W. L. Ames and, shortly afterward, of four other devoted members. These losses, historian Gannett noted, only made a closer bond between those who remained. On March 10, 1873, the original articles of association were replaced by the formal incorporation, under the state laws of Minnesota, of an organization to be known as "Unity Church"—the first Unitarian

---

[13] Kelley Journal, p. 38.
[14] Gannett, in Kelley Journal, p. 22.

church in this section of the country. (The name "Unity Church" is thought to have been originated by S. S. Hunting.) The list of trustees and incorporators included several of the original signers: John D. Ludden, Joseph S. Sewall, W. H. Kelley, Edmund R. Sewall, Edward Sawyer, Channing Seabury, James C. Boyden. The legal document of incorporation was certified by George A. Chapin and H. P. Grant.

Effinger, like most of the early ministers, had been taken on three months' trial, at the end of which he was given a permanent contract. Unity Church continued under his pastorate until June 19, 1876.

Little by little the young church was moving forward and managing to stay solvent. Finances were still its major problem, but it also had a minor one. That was the orthodox community's discomfort over and distrust of Unitarians. Back in 1858 the Swedish minister had offered family prayers on behalf of the handful of misguided unbelievers who were meeting over Pollock and Donaldson's Store. Mrs. Newell, wife of Frederick Newell, the former minister, had encountered numerous instances of antipathy. One lady, informed that her new neighbors were Unitarians, had exclaimed with holy horror "Oh dear! What ism will come next?" Another, a staunch Episcopalian, had told the rector of her church that she wanted to hear Newell preach. The rector graciously said that she might do so but enjoined her "to be careful not to listen to whatever he might preach and not to observe in what manner he might offer prayer." Again, in another Protestant church, the teacher of a Sunday school class of boys told them there were "three very bad sects in church worship—Universalists, Mormons, and Unitarians." The Universalists, she continued, were "quite bad," the Mormons were "very bad indeed," but the Unitarians were "the worst of all."[15]

With the Civil War over, the Unitarian Association in Boston had predicted, as already noted, a greater tolerance for

---

[15] Mrs. Frederick Newell To Mrs. Charles Clark, February 24, 1892, in Kelley Journal, p. 161.

Unitarian beliefs. But there was still plenty of antagonism against a group of people who not only scoffed at the Apostles' Creed but flaunted their rejection in the very name of their belief—Unitarianism. Effinger himself took cognizance of this disturbing influence when, in 1875, he wryly commented in a New Year's Day sermon:

> There are sufficient causes for our weakness, and one of these is the prejudice felt against us by the large majority of religious people—they deem us outlaws from the religious world, and the strong public sentiment which is thus brought to bear against us makes the timid fear to acknowledge their sympathy with us. There are many Unitarians in this city who are never seen in this church, who never give us the least aid or countenance, chiefly, I am persuaded, on this account. Social and business interests are too strong to be lightly risked.[16]

Little by little during Effinger's devoted pastorate the newly incorporated Unity Church surmounted its obstacles and managed to grow. Financial contributions of the members were now being supplemented from time to time by donations from the Association in Boston. By the summer of 1875 the Temperance Street building was becoming too small for church activities. By now the earlier Universalist dissension over Daniel Reed's liberalism had proven fatal, and the comparatively new church building on Wabasha stood vacant. The rental asked for its use was $1,000 per year. That was a large sum in 1875 and the expenditure of so much gave the Unitarians pause. Again, there was a great deal of discussion pro and con. We have Effinger's own account of the outcome:

> The matter was held in suspense—but at length Mr. O. P. Whitcomb, one of the Trustees, aided and abetted by his pastor, played the role of General Jackson and took the responsibility. The first Sunday of September 1875 found our congregation on the softly cushioned pews of the present house of worship. New faces appeared in the congregation. The church began to fill up surprisingly—but as the new year approached it was found that we

---

[16] Gannett, in Kelley Journal, p. 23.

were running in debt—that $400 and a little over were needed to square accounts. I presented the facts to the congregation and lo! in fifteen minutes nearly the whole sum was subscribed![17]

At least for the moment the financial crisis was over. But another misfortune awaited. Effinger had long been working in spite of weakened health. In March his condition became worse and he was able to preach only once more.

It was hoped that a leave of absence would restore him, but the vacation he took failed to bring back his strength and he was forced to tender his resignation. Gannett's account, from which we have already quoted, paid him this well-deserved tribute:

> It was the hardest blow the little church had known! Mr. Effinger's earnest, genial spirit had sowed the seed in a pretty wintry Spring.... The future ministers will reap a harvest that he planted for them![18]

So, Unity Church found itself without a pastor, barely solvent and with an expensive rental fee coming up month after month. For the next three months the Reverend W. J. Parrot, who had "preached himself out of" the Congregational Church of St. Paul by being too liberal, filled the pulpit of Unity Church. Then the Sunday services ceased, and the church again stood empty. But strength and purpose had crept into the Unitarians under Effinger's leadership and they immediately cast about industriously to find a successor. During the summer of 1876 Jenkin Lloyd Jones, a Unitarian minister and secretary of the Western Unitarian Conference, came to St. Paul to visit Effinger.[19] During his short stay Jones met with the St. Paul Unitarians, observed their strength and determination, and, to their great delight, informed them that he could put them in touch with "exactly the right man" for them. The man in question was the versatile William Channing Gannett of Boston,

---

[17] Gannett, in Kelley Journal, p. 26.
[18] Gannett, in Kelley Journal, p. 28.
[19] Jenkin Lloyd Jones was a lifelong friend of Gannett. He was minister of All Souls Church, Chicago in 1885; secretary of the Western Unitarian Conference, 1875-1884; and editor of *Unity*, 1880-1918.

who at that time did not have a parish, choosing to devote his time to writing the biography of his father.

Gannett was the first of the Unity Church ministers to be "born and bred" a Unitarian. His father, Ezra Stiles Gannett, was one of the founders of the American Unitarian Association, its first president, and a colleague and successor of William Ellery Channing, minister of the Federal Street Church (later called the Arlington Street Church) in Boston. The younger Gannett was born in Boston in 1840, graduated from Harvard in 1860, and subsequently taught school in Rhode Island. He then entered Harvard Divinity School. Finding himself beset with doubts as to either his ability to teach or his worthiness to be a minister, he interrupted his education to join the New England Freedman's Society, whose task it was to help the half-starving, neglected freed slaves on the islands off the coast of South Carolina. In spite of great hardships, including bouts with malaria, Gannett remained there for four years, in which time he managed plantations, opened schools, and devoted himself to what he felt was to be his life's work.

His father's poor health, however, forced him to return home. Later he accompanied the elder Gannett to Europe, remained there to study, and gradually resolved to resume his education for the ministry. His first parish (1868) was in Milwaukee, at that time a frontier town of muddy streets and wooden sidewalks, where doctors and ministers made their calls on horseback. In 1871, Gannett, feeling he should be near his ailing father, once again returned East, this time to a parish in East Lexington, Massachusetts. He had already begun writing the biography of his father. After Ezra Stiles Gannett's death, his son devoted himself to completing this work, some chapters of which are still regarded as a classic history of the evolution of American Unitarianism.

This man, now being considered for the ministry of Unity Church, was a true religious spirit, inspired all his life by the words and thoughts of Theodore Parker, Ralph Waldo Emerson, and William Ellery Channing, his godfather. To many contemporary Unitarians Gannett was a radical. Among other

18

things, he offended the conservatives by rewriting hymns and replacing the orthodox texts with new words. And, at a Cincinnati meeting of the Western Unitarian Conference in 1886, Gannett, with Jenkin Lloyd Jones as his ally, antagonized some members when he proposed the resolution that "the Conference conditions its fellowship on no dogmatic tests."[20] It was also noted with disapproval that the resolution contained no mention of the Christian heritage or allegiance.

Gannett was an ardent abolitionist and a strong woman suffragist. (Susan B. Anthony was his close friend and a fellow Unitarian.). Moreover, he was a passionate reformer, a born teacher, and above all, a parish minister. His son, Lewis Stiles Gannett, speaks of his father's "ever-inquiring clarity of mind, and the shining integrity of his character," and describes him as "a rarely modest man, friendly, if somewhat shy ... an impressive, radiant personality."[21] (A partial deafness probably contributed to his shyness.)

It was difficult for the small St. Paul group, with this account of Gannett's background, education, ability, and experience, to believe that there was any possibility of securing his services. Indeed, Kelley's record gives a clear picture of the discouraging plight of the local Unitarians at this time; the church and Sunday school were closed, and the situation seemed hopeless unless a man of Gannett's stature could be obtained to pull the group out of its doldrums.

It was difficult for the small St. Paul group, with this account of Gannett's background, education, ability, and experience, to believe that there was any possibility of securing his services. Indeed, Kelley's record gives a clear picture of the discouraging plight of the local Unitarians at this time; the church and Sunday school were closed, and the situation seemed hopeless

---

[20] Lewis S. Gannett, "William Channing Gannett," in *Heralds of a Liberal Faith* (Boston, 1925), IV, p. 144.
[21] Gannett, in Heralds of a Liberal Faith, IV, p. 146.

Figure 4 William Channing Gannett
Minister of Unity Church in St. Paul from 1877-1883
Approximately 1877
Minnesota Historical Society

unless a man of Gannett's stature could be obtained to pull the group out of its doldrums.

Joseph S. Sewall, chairman of the Board of Trustees, began a correspondence with Gannett, who, because of his stoutly held stand against any creed-making tendency and his outspoken liberal attitudes, felt compelled to lay his position before the members of Unity Church. His answer to Sewall, for transmittal to the St. Paul congregation, said in part, "You invite one unlikely to add to your numbers ... one, too, who can neither offer the Communion Service nor claim the 'Unitarian' or even the 'Christian' name, and who could attend your conferences only by the right of hearty interest, not of membership."[22] He went on to say that the American Unitarian Association must not be asked in any way to contribute to his salary, that he could not accept anything from that source, and he cautioned further that his hiring might otherwise influence the Association against the St. Paul church. "It is understood here," he said, "that one like me is fairly outside the denomination."

It is not surprising that this letter, expressing Gannett's unorthodox views and his feeling that he was not in good standing with his fellow Unitarians, caused great dismay and some opposition to his being called to Unity Church. After the members had deliberated, however, as to whether they could accept such a liberal thinker, Sewall wrote Gannett agreeing to his terms of $25 a week during the three months' trial ministry, and payment of his expenses from Boston and back again at the end of that period. After Gannett had preached his first sermon to a crowded church on March 25, 1877, and the congregation had met him, the opposition came to an end. At the conclusion of the three months he was rehired for a full year, at an annual salary of $1,800. The new minister, a bachelor, was thirty-seven years old when he began his pastorate.

Gannett was fortunate to find in his new congregation a closely bound group and strong individuals. Several members of this early time, many of whom have been mentioned, stand out not only as active church participants but also as distinct personalities.

One of the most interesting was Anderson H. Wimbish, an admirer of Gannett; so ardent was his admiration, in fact, that he is quoted as saying, "I divide all mankind into two classes; I

---

[22]William Channing Gannett to J.S. Sewell, February 4, 1877, in Kelley Journal, P. 57.

put Mr. Gannett in one, all the rest into another."[23] Wimbish was also a fervent crusader for the temperance movement, and played a large part in organizing such a group at Unity Church. He had a highly individualistic personality and was totally self-educated; it was through his avid, wide reading that he determined to leave his Methodist beliefs for Unitarianism.

Wimbish was born in Montgomery, Alabama, in 1826 and lived there until the outbreak of the Civil War, when, being pro-Union in his sentiments and having married a Northerner, Elizabeth Jamison, he came to St. Paul, a city recommended to him as "the healthiest spot in the world ... but some are doubtful of it as a place of business."[24] He had been a member of a printing firm in his native Montgomery and readily found work in the mailing room of the *St. Paul Pioneer.*

In 1901 he opened the Post Office Mission in his home on Laurel Avenue. This project consisted of mailing out religious literature to all who felt the need of liberal religion, and he requested his readers to spread the material around to others who had outgrown orthodox creeds. Wimbish undertook the labor and financial outlay himself, occasionally receiving donations from his readers, and, eventually, contributions from the church. The Mission was carried on for many years, but after 1940 there is no longer any mention of it.

From two sources, *A Family Chronicle* by Louise Bronson Crothers, the wife of Samuel McChord Crothers, and from reminiscences of a long-time church member, Mrs. Henry Sommers, we have entertaining descriptions of Wimbish. Mrs. Crothers writes, "He was a short little old man, with just a fringe of bushy white hair, blue eyes and rosy complexion."[25] Every Sunday, our informants tell us, Wimbish came to church—a little late because of his printer's duties—and took his accustomed place in the front seat of the side aisle. In cold weather he was enveloped in a big, shabby overcoat and a

---

[23] Richard W. Boynton, "An Unspotted Soul," in *Unity* LVIII (February 7, 1907), p. 450.
[24] Boynton, p. 451.
[25] Louise Bronson Crothers, *A Family Chronicle* (Concord, 1966), p. 117.

twenty-year-old knit chinchilla scarf, with fringes of all colors and literally yards long. After a short period, when sufficiently warmed, Wimbish would stand up, slowly unwind the scarf, layer after layer, then beamingly sit down again to listen to the service he loved. In 1902 the Board of Trustees allocated a $50 contribution to the American Unitarian Association for a life membership in honor of this devoted church member.

Two of the old families, united by the marriage of their children, were the Chapins and the Sewalls. In 1869 George A. Chapin brought his family to St. Paul from Boston, where they had been members of Edward Everett Hale's church. His daughter, Sarah, at the time of Unity Church's fiftieth anniversary in 1922, was the only member still living who had been one of the signers of the original church roster. Joseph S. Sewall, member of the first Board of Trustees, arrived from Boston in 1862. About twenty-four years later Gannett himself was especially summoned from Illinois to officiate at the wedding of Walter L. Chapin and Miss Mary Sewall. Mrs. Mary Chapin Heisig, third-generation church member, in reminiscing of her maternal grandfather, relates that in the winter of 1905 Sewall's house burned down. The following day, the elderly gentleman announced that "anyway he saved the *Christian Register*," the official Unitarian magazine of its day.[26]

The names of Mr. and Mrs. Charles H. Clark, co-signers of the first membership list of 1859, are found throughout the church records in varied capacities. Clark, also a native of Boston, was a hardware merchant and in the early days in St. Paul lived in a log cabin on Ramsey Street. He and his wife were dedicated church members and lifelong generous contributors. It is to Martha Clark that Unity Church is indebted for most of the papers on Wimbish and many other documents relating to church history.

---

[26] Mrs. George B. Heisig to Elinor s. Otto, February 10, 1970.

Figure 5 Mrs. C. Clarke
Meadville Lombard Archives

Another pioneer in the liberal religious movement in the
Northwest and a staunch supporter of Unity Church was Orlan
P. Whitcomb. He was a native of New York State, but began his
career as a teacher in Wisconsin. He eventually settled in
Minnesota where he held several public offices including those
of member of the Board of Education, president of the State
Agricultural Society, and, in 1872, state auditor. He was
instrumental in organizing the Minneapolis Unitarian Society
and was one of the most active trustees and builders of the
church under Gannett.

Among the many additional loyal Unitarians of this time were
the Baileys, the DeGraws, and the Sawyers. Everett Bailey was
president of the First National Bank, 1907-18, and both he and
his wife entered into every phase of church life. The same can
be said of the DeGraws, who lived just in back of the Wabasha
Street church and whose lives centered there in the
companionship of their fellow Unitarians. Edward Sawyer, who
came from Concord, New Hampshire, and became treasurer of
the Great Northern Railroad, was also a charter member of the
group and often substituted in the pulpit when the church was
without a minister.

Much to the satisfaction of Unity Church parents, it was soon discovered that one of the new minister's prime interests was the Sunday school, which Gannett immediately re-established, serving as its superintendent himself. The St. Paul Unitarians had early felt the importance of religious education for their children, and, under Effinger, well-attended classes had been held regularly. During the period between Effinger's resignation and Gannett's arrival, these classes had been abandoned. So, the prompt action in restoring them was welcomed.

During 1878—the first full calendar year of Gannett's ministry—the Sunday school, staffed by seventeen teachers, reached an average attendance of eighty-six. Beginning at 12:15, following the close of the church service, it consisted of a children's choral service, a short address by Gannett, and class lessons. Gannett himself wrote all the lessons and study outlines for his own classes and sent copies to other Unitarian churches because, in his opinion, those published in Boston, the only source of such material at this time, were unsatisfactory. For many years these Sunday school lessons were widely used by most Unitarian churches. Financial support of the Sunday school at Unity depended upon the "Children's Penny" brought each Sunday, by the church collection of the first Sunday of each month, and by special donations.

Under Gannett's direction there was, within the Sunday school, an emphasis on "good works." The Lend A Hand Club distributed Thanksgiving baskets to the needy, Christmas gifts to the children in an orphanage, and Sunday school papers written by Gannett to a church school in Georgia.[27] Temperance played an important part in the church school teaching of this era, and the children had their own temperance society, known as the True Helpers.[28] The goal of

---

[27] The name was derived from a motto in *The Rule of the "Harry Wadsworth Club,"* by Edward Everett Hale.
[28] The inclusion of children in the temperance organization dates back to 1847 in Leeds, England.

this group, open to anyone over eight years old, was "to train the young in Public Spirit, Temperance and Honor." Members took a pledge to give up alcohol, the pledge to be renewed every three months, and each member was given a white silk badge adorned with the motto "For Their Sake and Honor." The president of this, to our modern viewpoint, astounding children's organization, was A. H. Wimbish.

A delightful group, known as Q.F.U., standing for Quick-Fingered-Unit, was open to all the church's boys and girls (and to their friends over eleven years old, until increasing popularity and lack of space necessitated holding down the membership to one hundred). The Q.F.U. met Saturday afternoons. Its activities included manual training for the boys, and sewing and painting for the girls, and concluded with dancing lessons for all.

Figure 6
"True Helpers" Badge
In William Channing
Gannett's scrapbook,
Minnesota Historical
Society

As one marvels at the multifold programs mentioned in the church bulletins of the late 1800's, and at the zealous co-operation and participation on the part of the congregation, young and old, one is reminded that few recreational facilities were available in this era and that a large share of the social life of the time centered in the church. In 1881-82, after four years of Gannett's pastorate, we find the following organizations making their contributions:

> Unity Club, which was organized in 1877, was second in importance only to church services and Sunday school. It was, to quote the 1885 Unity Church Yearbook," For improvement and entertainment; the social and

educational life of the church."[29] Membership was open to everyone connected with the church and to any interested friends outside it. The first officers were Edward Sawyer, president, and Mrs. Samuel J. Beals, Jr., secretary and treasurer. The programs consisted of study classes on cultural subjects, for which the members themselves wrote papers, as well as musical evenings and amateur dramatics. A Flower Mission, to distribute fruits and flowers to the hospitals, and the children's Q.F.U., already mentioned, were among the branches of Unity Club.

The Ladies Benevolent Society was begun in 1876, prior to Gannett's coming, and continued actively throughout his pastorate. The group endeavored to help needy women by providing them with both work and clothing. The women were hired as seamstresses and the garments they made were given to the poor or sold inexpensively at the society's Thursday meetings. Mrs. Charles Clark was the first president.

In addition to these organizations, the church, under the heading of "city relief work," appointed a representative to each of the following St. Paul institutions: Home for the Friendless, Protestant Orphan Asylum, St. Paul Relief Society, and Woman's Christian Home.

Almost exactly two years after Gannett's arrival a significant event occurred. Apparently by his own free choice and not because of any strong opposition to his liberal views on the part of the Unitarians, Gannett was as yet unordained. On March 2, 1879, he requested his St. Paul congregation to ordain him as their minister, which they gladly did the following Sunday. Jenkin Lloyd Jones presided at the ceremony and preached the sermon. At the end of the ordination ceremony, Gannett read an "agreement" written by him to be signed by members of the congregation to signify affiliation with the church. This is an interesting incident, considering Gannett's earlier firm stand

---

[29] Unity Church Yearbook, 1885, p. 15.

against any statement resembling a creed. He explained, however, that though his words did constitute a creed of sorts, it was "one made up not of the intellectual beliefs, but of the principles and ideals of our religion."[30] This "agreement," written nearly one hundred years ago, is still in use. It can be found in the first pages of the membership book, and, as the "Bond of Fellowship," is an integral part of the ceremony of joining the church, when it is spoken in unison by the congregation and the new members. Gannett's statement reads:

> As those who believe in Religion,
> As those who believe in Freedom, Fellowship and Character in Religion,
> As those who believe that the religious life means the thankful, trustful, loyal and helpful life,
> And as those who believe that a church is a brotherhood of helpers wherein it is made easier to lead such a life,
> We join ourselves together, name, hand and heart as members of Unity Church.

Subsequently the Board of Trustees filed the proper certificate of ordination with the Ramsey County Registry of Deeds. Gannett now had official state approval to perform marriages. The first one to be recorded in Kelley's journal was that of Frank B. Jilson to Miss Caroline A. Beals.

Gannett was far ahead of his time in conceiving of the church as a "Family of Families," and allied with this concept was his dream of church ownership of a "home." As 1879 progressed, there arose increasingly within the congregation a similar hope. The rented Universalist Church was still adequate, but its owner was anxious to sell. At about this time some desirable lots further up on Wabasha Street, at the foot of Summit Avenue, became available and could be purchased reasonably. (This site is now a part of the capitol grounds on the east side of Wabasha, just north of Interstate 94.) Four men of the congregation—Edward Sawyer, O. P. Whitcomb, J. S. Sewall,

---

[30] Kelley Journal, p. 73.

and J. D. Ludden—assumed the responsibility of making the purchase.

Before deciding to build there, however, the church made an offer of $13,000 for the Universalist Church property. Since the asking price remained too high, $17,000, the church members decided in favor of building. They appointed a Building Committee consisting of Ludden, chairman, Sewall, Mrs. F. P. Sawyer, Mrs. Charles Clark, and Gannett.

Figure 7 Mr. and Mrs. Edward Sawyer

Mrs. Sawyer, 1879   Edward Sawyer, May 1885.
Meadville Lombard Archives   Meadville Lombard Archives

Several things needed to be done before hiring an architect. A subscription paper was circulated among the members, stipulating that the building project would be considered only if $6,000 were subscribed, no debt of over $3,000 to be incurred for the lots and building. Originally the pledges amounted to only $4,400, substantially below the goal. And now Gannett took advantage of a heart-warming incident. Soon after the news had filtered back to Boston of Unity Church's hopes for a building of its own, an unsolicited check for $100 came from Miss Anne D. Williams, an elderly friend of Gannett's father. This was a tribute to Ezra Stiles Gannett's memory, and his son realized that there might be more of his father's former devoted parishioners who would be happy to share in such a tribute. During the summer he wrote to other friends in his father's parish, telling them of his hopes and plans.

By September 1879, the St. Paul pledges amounted to $5,915. Gannett's personal letter alone brought in $1,230. Eventually this figure grew to over $7,000, one-third of the final cost of the church property. To reach this surprising figure several of Ezra Stiles Gannett's elderly parishioners, including the venerable Anne Williams, had turned themselves into eager solicitors.

In Gannett's own words we have this account of what followed:
> We carefully planned the inside of the Church to suit our various social needs, and asked the architects to cover this inside with an outside that should express the same idea, that of a Church Home, adapting to a church in some simple form the picturesque 'Queen Anne' style, so called, of house architecture.[31]

The result is the cottage church we have, which has so puzzled the good people of the city, and so well satisfied ourselves."[32]

With the architect's plans completed, three contractors' bids were submitted and the job awarded to the low bidder— G. W. Merrill—at a figure of $9,687. And now a bit of bad luck came along. The rented church was sold to a French Catholic group. There was nothing to do but go back to a rented hall (this time Sherman Hall, on the corner of Sixth and Wabasha) until the new building was completed.

---

[31] The architect was coincidentally named Wiliam Ellery Channing Whitney, of the Minneapolis firm of Plan and Whitney.
[32] Gannett, in Kelley Journal, p. 98

Construction work began May 31, 1880, but almost immediately another misfortune struck. The hole which the workmen were digging for the basement promptly filled up with water. Before progressing farther a drainage ditch had to be dug, with special permission, through a neighboring lot. Once the hole drained, the cause of the trouble was only too evident. An unsuspected peat bed underlay the property. For an adequate foundation piling had to be driven and a broad base of heavy stone and cement grouting installed.

All this took extra time and money. The harassed contractor watched all hope of profit disappearing, then all hope of avoiding serious loss, and finally all hope of covering his mounting expenses. Of these trials Gannett wrote:

> The chairman of the building committee resigned November 21. ... The contractor failed December 10, insolvent, and left his half-finished building on our hands. ... The chimneys tumbled down. The gas-fitters sent a drinking workman to do their work and much of it had to be done over. The plasterers had to do their work in zero weather. The price of materials was rising. There was no effective supervision after the contractor's failure; honest and sorry, he looked after the job awhile, then left the city.[33]

More money was badly needed. The women of the church gave a Christmas fair that brought in almost $1,000. Some of the church members, including Martha Clark, appealed to their Unitarian friends in other cities for donations, and St. Paul friends outside the church contributed $700. The $3,000 permitted under the terms of the subscription was so difficult to borrow that finally a loan was accepted from Mrs. Charles Clark, Mrs. Edward Sawyer, and Gannett himself. old friends in the East were again appealed to and generously sent an additional $1,350. And so, in early 1882, Gannett was able to report:

> "The Annual Church Meeting... on Jan. 28th, 1882... was held in the new building, its first use. Only the lower

---

[33] Gannett, in Kelley Journal, p.99.

floor was ready—upstairs was still chaos—we pledged ourselves again for quarterly payments—$2511 in all. And the next day (Jan. 29th, 1882) we spent our first glad Sunday in our Church-Home. The service all through must have reflected the thoughts and the thanksgivings in our hearts, and they made our simple dedication."[34]

Little by little over the next two years, as new subscriptions and gifts permitted, the inside of the church was finished and partially equipped. A second Christmas fair brought in $900 and with this the congregation felt at liberty to order the pews, which were to be of butternut, and the pulpit, of cherry wood. Vines and trees were planted outside, gas fixtures installed inside, and all the available inside space, including the attic, made usable. The historic ice-water barrel, with its tin cup hanging on a chain, was set in place on the street in front of the church. At the very outset this barrel became a symbol not only of good neighbor policy to all parched passers-by, but of the belief in the desirability of clear, ice-cold water as compared to the frothy brew obtainable in the saloon on the corner. And, good Temperance Society members that they were, the True Helpers contributed their small fees to support this project. However, it is nowhere a matter of record how many, if any, of the Wabasha Street loiterers were diverted from the saloon by the lure of the water barrel.

In every way, the new building, planned from the inside out, suited its proud owners. It came into use, one way or another, four or five days of every week. Its lower floor served perfectly for "all the social services, the games of the children, the evening tea with one another, the lecture, the discussion, the dramatics, the concert or the dance. The rear room served as a Public Reading Room on Sunday afternoons."[35] The parlor took care of teachers' meetings, the study club, and the Benevolent Society. The audience room housed the church services.

---

[34] Gannett, in Kelley Journal, p.100.
[35] Gannett, in Kelley Journal, p. 101.

Figure 8 The "Queen Anne" Church on Wabasha Street. Circa 1890
Minnesota Historical Society

Figure 9 Unity Church, Wabasha Street, Appr. 1900
Minnesota Historical Society

In spite of the great joy Gannett and his parishioners found in their new edifice, at least three members of the congregation have expressed quite different viewpoints. In recent interviews Miss Eleanor Jilson recalled it as an ugly, uninviting building and Miss Mary Davis remembered that, as a child, she was not allowed to attend Sunday school at all, because it was such a damp and unhealthy place; Mrs. Crothers, the wife of a later minister, found the "Queen Anne" cottage an unimposing building, which, however, she remembered with affection.

The first half of 1883 brought a well-earned satisfaction to the people of Unity Church. They now owned a substantial, well-located property. It had cost over $23,000, far more than had originally been contemplated. But it was free of indebtedness except for that easily managed $3,000 mortgage. There was growing respect within the city for the unorthodox denomination and the courage and loyalty of its members. (The list of "outside friends" who had contributed to the church building fund included the name of James J. Hill.) The cement grouting which covered the peat bed had put a firm foundation under the church structure. And Gannett's organizational and administrative talents had put an even firmer foundation under the entire church itself. It was self-supporting, alive with activities for its members, and proud of its accomplishments.

And then, in midsummer, during the annual vacation, occurred the still faintly inexplicable resignation of Gannett. It came July 29, 1883, in a letter he wrote answering one from the trustees seeking the renewal of his pastorate for another year. In the absence of any other explanation we have only these words from that letter:

> It is nearly a month since the people invited me to stay another year. ... It has been a hard question to decide. A great deal of friendship and pleasure and a feeling that the church would go on fairly well with me as minister lie on one side; a strong wish to stop regular work of this kind 'til I feel again more like it, meanwhile doing some other things that have long been waiting, and the belief that a new minister might do more for the church than I,

lie on the other side. ... And now ... I write you to decline, with many thanks and much love, the new invitation.[36]

The distressed congregation could not accept the situation without another try. It adopted and forwarded a resolution urging Gannett to reconsider, to take a leave of absence and then return. In his reply Gannett pointed out that such a year of temporary pastorates would be merely marking time when the church should be moving forward, and he again declined.

So the church lost a pastor who was also poet, hymn writer, preacher, organizer, administrator, builder, and fund raiser. In due course Gannett served for a time as minister of the Unitarian Church in Hinsdale, Illinois, then minister-at-large for the Western Unitarian Conference. From there he moved on to his remarkable nineteen-year active pastorate of the First Unitarian Church of Rochester, New York, and an additional fifteen years as minister emeritus. At the age of forty-seven he married Mary Thorn Lewis, a Quaker, who became his able assistant. By the time of his death in 1923, he had become, in the words of one of his many eulogists, "The beloved seer, poet and saint of the liberal religious fellowship."[37] At a later date Frederick Eliot paid this tribute to him: "There have been many ministers of Unity Church since Mr. Gannett's day, and some of them have been notable servants of the truth; but all of them would gladly acknowledge that they have built on his foundations."[38]

During Gannett's successful ministry, he had fulfilled at least two of his three personal hopes for his St. Paul church: a "home" had been erected, a church history had been written by his own hand, and a chronicler, the faithful William Kelley, had been found to continue the task. Only the establishment of a choir as

---

[36] William Channing Gannett to Edward Sawyer, July 29, 1882, in Kelley Journal, p. 110.
[37] Charles W. Wendte, "Memories of William Channing Gannett,"in Unity, XCIII (March 6, 1924), p. 9.
[38] Frederick M. Eliot, "Samuel McChord Crothers," in *Heralds of a Liberal Faith* (Boston, 1952), IV, p. 107.

an integral part of the Sunday service was postponed until a future date.

Figure 10 William Channing Gannett, about 1910
Minister of Unity Church, 1877-1883
Minnesota Historical Society

III. "A Family of Families" 1884-1900

The fifteen-year period following Gannett's departure was characterized, with one notable exception, by brief and not always satisfactory pastorates. Within this space of time Unity Church had five different ministers. In spite of this the church grew stronger.

Of course it could not be hoped that the congregation would immediately find another such leader as Gannett. Jenkin Lloyd Jones and Gannett himself were members of the committee to choose a new minister. Although the pastorate was offered to Jones, he was not interested. The successor to Gannett finally selected was Clay MacCauley, who, in October 1884, began a six months' trial ministry at Unity Church. The following April he accepted a contract for an additional year.

Of all the ministers of the St. Paul church, MacCauley had the most varied career. Born in 1843 in Chambersburg, Pennsylvania, he was reared a Calvinist, and as quite a young man he determined to become a Presbyterian minister. He served in the Civil War, distinguishing himself for outstanding bravery, and he endured great hardship as a prisoner of war. Later, while serving a church in Wisconsin, he again questioned the doctrines of his religion and finally turned to Unitarianism. He accepted a call from a Unitarian church in Morrison, Illinois, but found that there his beliefs were considered heretical.

Succeeding Gannett would have been difficult for anyone, but other circumstances contributed to an inauspicious beginning for MacCauley's ministry. He felt, and quite frankly said so, that the $1,500 salary was highly inadequate. In addition, his conception of what a ministry should be did not coincide with that of his congregation. According to a letter from Frederick Jackson to Mrs. Charles Clark (March 1, 1885), MacCauley displayed great aptitude for organization. Through advertisements in the Sunday papers and through speaking engagements he brought Unity Church very prominently to the public notice. He carried on the various activities within the church, but his most absorbing interest was in establishing Unitarianism as a great and widespread religious movement. To further this goal of making his religion understood and accepted throughout the community, MacCauley took advantage of every opportunity to speak at meetings outside the church and to deal in his sermons with the social ills of the times.

Unfortunately, these activities brought about a sharp cleavage between those members of the congregation who approved of this type of ministry and those who did not. The latter group felt that in concentrating on social problems MacCauley was neglecting the spiritual problems of his parishioners. The cleavage widened as the time approached for renewing his one-year contract, and it threatened to split the church. On April 9, 1886, ninety-eight petitioners signed a statement in favor of extending the contract. But a membership vote was so close that MacCauley, with the best interests of the church at heart, and feeling that only he could stop the dissension, quietly withdrew. So Unity Church was again without a minister.

After returning to New England MacCauley was appointed to a mission in Japan where he spent twenty-one years as a teacher, counselor to Japanese liberals, preacher, writer, and editor.

The unfortunate outcome of MacCauley's brief one-and one-half-year pastorate was summed up in Kelley's chronicle. The account quotes a Boston clergyman who, after Gannett's resignation, predicted wryly to a visiting St. Paulite that "your society would build an altar and sacrifice on it the next applicant for the pulpit." And Kelley himself succinctly added, "Mr. MacCauley was the victim."[39]

Despite the division within the church membership, one heartening thing had occurred during MacCauley's tenure. The $3,000 mortgage on the church was paid off. Credit for this was

---

[39] Kelley Journal, p. 152.

due largely to the generosity of John D. Ludden, who, at the January annual meeting had offered to pay one third of the debt if the remainder was raised by the first of April.

Fortunately the rift over MacCauley did not widen. In fact, it started closing when the fortuitous choice of a successor again brought to Unity Church an outstanding minister: one who was to serve a seven-year popular and successful pastorate and was to leave only when a great opportunity called him east again.

This new minister was Samuel McChord Crothers. He was only twenty-nine years old (and looked even younger) when he came to St. Paul from Brattleboro, Vermont, in September of 1886 to preach at two Sunday services. Such was the enthusiasm aroused by Crothers' personality and his sermons that he was immediately offered, not the customary three months' trial, but a term of engagement of no less than one year, on the understanding that the contract could then be terminated on three months' notice by the pastor or the congregation.

Crothers accepted the offer, pulled up his New England roots, and began his ministerial duties in St. Paul on October 17, 1886.

Born in Oswego, Illinois, in 1857, Crothers came from a staunchly Presbyterian Scottish family. He was graduated from Wittenberg College in Ohio, but since he was only sixteen at the time, he took an additional year of study, receiving an A.B. degree from Princeton University. Intent on becoming a Presbyterian minister he attended Union Theological Seminary and after his ordination spent two years in the mission field in Nevada. His next move was to California, where he filled a pulpit at Santa Barbara and where he met his future wife, Louise M. Bronson, who proved to be a perfect helpmate in his ministerial work.

This was a happy period in Crothers' life, and he developed tremendously as a preacher and a minister. It gradually became apparent to his parishioners, however, that he was no longer preaching sound Presbyterian doctrine. When challenged on this point by uneasy members of his congregation, Crothers replied in his typically gentle manner that "he was preaching, not the doctrines peculiar to Presbyterianism, but the doctrines wherein Presbyterianism was in accord with Christianity."[40] Finally recognizing that his religious thinking was in a transitional stage, he withdrew from the Presbyterian church. He returned East to resume study at Harvard Divinity School and then entered the Unitarian ministry.

In time Crothers became particularly noted for his sermons and prayers and, being an outstanding lecturer and having enormous appeal to young people, he was much in demand at colleges and universities throughout the country. The benign humor, the wit devoid of malice and the shrewd observations which made his lectures so popular were equally evident in his delightful essays. An excessive shyness hampered Crothers as a parish minister, but the excellence of his preaching was compensation enough for his parishioners.

Crothers had a magnificent mind but frequently became preoccupied with his own thoughts to the exclusion of more practical matters. Wallace Robbins (a later minister of Unity Church) tells this anecdote. The parsonage was heated with "parlor stoves" and Crothers constantly had to be reminded when they needed filling. On one occasion Mrs. Crothers, after waiting some time for her husband to return from the basement with the coal, at length went in search of him. He was pacing up and down, carrying the full coal hod in one hand, while he continued to read from the book he had taken with him. Another characteristic was viewed lightly by the congregation. Mary Davis relates that the opening hymn at every Sunday service was "Holy, Holy, Holy." The reason for this, Crothers later confessed, was that he was tone-deaf, and this hymn and "My Country 'Tis of Thee" were the only tunes he could recognize. But the mild, shy impression he made belied a

---

[40] Eliot, "Samuel McChord Crothers," in *Heralds of a Liberal Faith*, p.107.

Figure 11 Samuel McChord Crothers
Minister of Unity Church, 1886-1894

moral toughness, because he was also a man of firm
convictions, and one who unhesitantly defended many
unpopular causes.

The first fine impression the youthful minister made on his St.
Paul congregation was not matched by the impression their
new surroundings made on the minister's family. Mrs.

Crothers, especially, was struck by the ugliness of this young city where she was now to live. Louise Bronson Crothers, in *A Family Chronicle*, relates that her mother, accustomed to the elm-shaded, winding streets of New England towns, was depressed by the "rectangular streets, with miles of wooden sidewalks, and rows of little whisps [sic], of trees four or six feet high and little two-by-six-room houses."[41] But the initial disappointments, even the constant struggle to maintain a family of five on the minister's meager salary of $1,500 (later raised to $2,500, which then seemed like comparative wealth), did not prevent the development of a deep attachment between the Crothers family and their fellow church members. In Louise Crothers' words, "The St. Paul Parish was small enough and spiritually isolated enough to draw us very close together.... Never were people so kind, so expressive and affectionate."[42] Some years later an even stronger tie with St. Paul was formed by the marriage of Charles Ames's daughter, Alice, to Bronson Crothers, the minister's son.

At this juncture, Unity Church was making steady progress in most areas. The records list about one hundred and twenty subscribers. The treasurer's report for September 1885, shows that the annual subscriptions amounted to $1,933.12, Sunday collections came to $141.57, and in addition approximately $550 was raised by fairs and dramatic entertainments. The total cost of maintaining the church was $2,826.37. The list of contributors and active members still contained names of the original Unitarian group, while, of course, new ones were being added.

The Sunday school was also gaining ground, with a small increase in the average attendance. Charles W. Ames was the superintendent at this time, and in his report for the year 1885, he gives the following information. The total enrollment stood at eighty-four. There were twelve teachers, all but one of them female. The lessons in use were the *Teachings of Jesus*, published by the Unitarian Sunday School Society of Boston,

---

[41] Crothers, A Family Chronicle, p. 114.
[42] Crothers, A Family Chronicle, p. 113.

which currently was the only good source of material. These texts replaced many of the lessons that had been written by Gannett during his St. Paul ministry.

An influential part of the church school was its library, which, by 1877, consisted of four hundred books. There was even a small catalogue in pamphlet form. A church member has testified to the tremendous importance these books played in the lives of the children. Mrs. Henry Sommers remembers that:

> taking out a book meant Sunday School to me. Tucked away at the very back of the lower floor of the Wabasha Street church was the Library. ... Each book was covered with thick, shiny, cream-colored wrapping paper, the name of the book printed on the back in black ink.[43]

By 1897 the library report showed that forty-five children were reading the books regularly, and that a total of six hundred and forty-six books were taken out in one year. Three of the librarians mentioned at various times were H. D. McGraw, Miss Jessie Ware, and Miss Mabel Kendrick, all remembered for faithfulness to their task.

Gannett, together with his desires for a church "home" and a church chronicle, had harbored hopes for music led by a proficient and steady choir. But throughout the early years, this seemed impossible to achieve with any degree of success or regularity. By 1885 a choir was available, if not highly satisfactory, since the annual report states that the Board of Trustees "deemed it advisable ... to dispense with the choir, and depend, instead, upon the congregation for the musical part of the services."[44] It was through the efforts of the organist, Miss Susan Beals, the report continues, that "in bringing the musical members of our society together for rehearsal ... a marked improvement has been made in rendering the hymns and responses."

In 1888 an Organ Fund Association was established and a contract made with Hook and Hastings of Boston to build an

---

43 Mrs. Henry Sommers to Elinor S. Otto, July 13, 1969.
44 Unity Church Yearbook 1885, p. 15.

organ at the top price of $2,000. The women of the church, who had already advanced a loan, without interest, for this project, now raised the necessary final amount of $1,750 by means of their annual fairs in the years 1887-90.

At the time of Crothers' arrival in St. Paul, the most vigorous organizations continued to be the True Helpers, the Ladies Benevolent Society, the Post Office Mission, and Unity Club. The latter, now presided over by Charles W. Ames, went on offering programs of "improvement and entertainment." The church was still the social and intellectual center of activity, and members of Unity Church were entertaining themselves and their friends with musicals, parties, and amateur dramatics.

For instance, on March 4, 1884, you could have seen a performance of "The Flower of the Family: A Comedy in Three Acts"; or for fifty cents, on May 31, 1889, a program consisting of "A Medical Man: A Farce," by W. S. Gilbert, starring two of the Ames clan and F. L. Kellogg, plus songs by the Misses Van Gelder and Della Long. And, if you had been fortunate enough to be on hand in May of 1890, you could have witnessed an extravaganza, put on by the inventive Ames, of an exhibition of wax works. In fact, the production, advertised as "amusing, instructive, awful ... for all ages and sexes," was such a success that a repeat performance was requested.

In sharp contrast to the tolerance shown for all this lively weekday entertainment is the attitude of Unitarians towards programs presented in the church on Sundays. In 1890 Kristofer Janson,[45] who was attempting to organize Unitarian societies among the Norwegian population of St. Paul, had been given permission to hold a Sunday evening meeting in the church on Wabasha Street. His request for a second meeting

---

[45] Norwegian and Lutheran by birth, Janson adopted Unitarianism and in 1881 was invited by the American Unitarian Association to establish missions in Minnesota. He organized Unitarian groups in Minneapolis, St. Paul, Hanska, and Underwood, Minnesota, and in Hudson, Wisconsin. In 1893, he returned to Norway, where he established a Unitarian society in Christiana, serving as its pastor until his death.

was denied, however, because of the musical selections presented on the first occasion. In reponse to this refusal Janson sent an irate letter to the Unity Church Board of Trustees in which he wrote:

> We did not dream... that the Trustees of Unity Church were so ignorant of musical affaires [sic] as not to know that Chopin's waltzes and mazurkas are not dancing music at all—but classical music played at all your so-called sacred concerts."[46]

The trustees were not swayed: Chopin's dances and Janson were refused admittance.

Any portrayal of the Unity Church of that day is not complete without the story of Charles Wilberforce Ames, whose name appears so frequently here. Ames's father, Charles Gordon Ames, was the adopted son of a New Hampshire family. He began his career as a Baptist minister, but left his home and his Baptist beliefs behind him, settled in Minneapolis, and turned to the Unitarian ministry. He was at one time the editor of the *Christian Register*.

The second Ames, Charles Wilberforce, was born in 1855 in Minneapolis, was graduated from Cornell University with a Phi Beta Kappa key, and eventually became the president of West Publishing Company in St. Paul. For thirty-eight years he played such a vital role in Unity Church that his contributions cannot be calculated. Among the numerous positions he held were trustee, Sunday school superintendent, first president of the Laymen's League, and president of the Minnesota Unitarian Conference. He was a generous contributor, an instigator of many of the social activities of the church, and, in any emergency, it was to him that the minister and the congregation turned. In addition he was a commanding figure in the business, social, and intellectual life of the community.

In speaking to Ames's contemporaries one hears of his unquenchable vitality and gaiety, his keen sense of humor, his

---

46 Kristofer Janson to the Board of Trustees of Unity Church, November 28, 1890.

love of showmanship, and a responsiveness that attracted everyone to him. A story, recalled by Wallace Robbins, indicates that Ames, in spite of his loyalty to Gannett, did not share the minister's firm convictions about the evils of alcohol. As a boy, Ames's son, Lesley, accompanied his father to the temperance meetings at the church. On leaving one of these lectures the senior Ames discreetly closed the church door behind him, and stood silent on the steps for a moment. He then raised his arms, shouted "Give me rum!" and jumped into a waist-high snow bank.

Ames's wife, Mary, was also a much beloved, serene person, about whom Louise Crothers wrote, "She contributed out of all proportion the spirit that makes and keeps a church worthwhile. ...She never seemed busy, though I never saw her idle."[47] A number of progeny in the Ames family continues into the third generation of St. Paul Unitarians.

Often mentioned in the records of this time, too, were the Tiffanys, another family originating in Massachusetts. The senior Francis Tiffany was a Unitarian minister who later substituted in the Unity Church pulpit for Richard Boynton. Young Francis came to St. Paul with his wife, Nina, in 1890 and continued his law practice here. Mrs. Tiffany was the author of two books on the early leaders of the Unitarian movement. One was a biography of Harm Jan Huidekoper, founder of Meadville Theological School, and the other, *Pathbreakers*, was published in 1949. Mrs. Tiffany was then over ninety years old and lived on to attain the great age of one hundred and six.

Among other names prominent in the annals of the church is that of Dr. William Davis, chairman of the Board of Trustees from 1892-94. This family also brought its New England heritage to St. Paul, and nicely links together some well-known Unitarians. Mrs. Davis was not only a cousin of William Channing Gannett, but also the sister of Thomas Gannett Holyoke, the architect of the original Portland and Grotto church. The Davis' son, Holyoke, was for a time a member of

---

[47] Cothers, *A Family Chronicle*, p. 122.

46

the architectural firm of Holyoke, Jemne, and Davis, and their daughter, Mary, has been for many years an active member of the church.

Under Crothers we find the St. Paul Unitarians taking a wider interest in their Minnesota Unitarian neighbors. During the summer of 1887, when the auditorium of the new Minneapolis church had finally been finished, the St. Paulites accepted an invitation to attend the first service held there. In November of that same year, a number of the Unitarians of Minnesota met in Unity Church for the purpose of organizing the Minnesota Conference. The new organization held its first meeting in April 1888, in Sioux Falls, Dakota Territory, with Crothers present as a delegate.[48] And still later in the year, when the Minnesota Conference held a second meeting in St. Cloud, the contingent from St. Paul included the minister and three official delegates as well as nine additional members of Unity Church. An interesting indication of the spread of Unitarianism throughout the state was the fact that attending the meeting were delegates not only from St. Paul, Minneapolis, and Duluth, but also from Winona, St. Cloud, Luverne, Sioux Falls, and Alma, Wisconsin.

Early in 1892 the stalwarts of the church outlined plans for a fitting celebration of its twentieth anniversary. Crothers suggested a Sunday service at which Gannett, Effinger, S. S. Hunting (Western Conference head), and Jenkin Lloyd Jones would be guests. February 28 was selected and the ceremony was a great success. Of those invited only Effinger and Jones were unable to come. Crothers read the opening service, Hunting delivered the prayer, and Gannett preached the sermon. According to Kelley, who always paid due attention to the weather that accompanied church events, "It was ushered in with a fine display of the Aurora Borealis."[49] At the dinner the following night Charles Ames presided as master of

---

[48] The Minnesota Conference at this time included Sioux Falls, Aberdeen, Huron, Minot in Dakota Territory, and Madison in Wisconsin. (North and South Dakota did not become states until 1889.)
[49] Kelley Journal, p. 158.

ceremonies and, as Kelley again notes, "set off a few rhetorical pyrotechnics in his happiest mood."

During this time the news was spreading in Unitarian circles about Crothers' fruitful ministry of Unity Church. In March, only a month after the twentieth anniversary celebration, he received a call from the prestigious Arlington Street Church in Boston at a salary slightly more than twice as much as he was receiving in St. Paul. He declined the call and continued at Unity Church through January 1894. Then he received a second call, this time to the First Parish Church in Cambridge, Massachusetts. This invitation, offering an opportunity to work with Harvard University students, was so attractive that he found himself unable to refuse it. His letter of resignation expresses his feelings:

> With deep regret over the necessity of breaking ties that have bound me here, I write to present my resignation. ... I have long been convinced that there was the possibility of a work being done by the Unitarian minister in Cambridge of peculiar importance and urgency. To adequately impress any considerable portion of the young men at the university with the vital power of liberal religion would give to our cause the kind of reinforcement it greatly needs. At no other point did it seem to me that there was such an opportunity to influence not simply the present but also the future. ...
>
> To reject it would be for me to reject the opportunity of doing the largest service which my own judgment tells me I could do for Unitarianism in America. ... I need not tell you at what cost this decision is made."[50]

Recognizing the validity of Crothers' decision, the St. Paul congregation regretfully accepted his resignation. In a resolution passed at a special meeting, the membership acknowledged its great debt to him for the many accomplishments of his ministry.

---

[50] Samuel M. Crothers to the Board of Trustees of Unity Church, February 3, 1894 in Kelley Journal, p. 178.

Crothers served a thirty-three-year pastorate at the First Parish Church and remained in Cambridge until his death in 1927. Recognition came to him generously, as attested to by the awards he received from universities, including a D.D. from Harvard, and a Litt.D. from St. Lawrence, Canton, New York.

The pattern for securing a new minister was, by now, fairly well standardized. Each Sunday the pulpit was filled by a different minister, borrowed from a nearby church, or available in the area from the ranks of the Western Conference in Chicago or of the American Unitarian Association in Boston. In addition, there was a handful of actual prospects for the job whom the denomination was careful not to embarrass by labeling "candidates." There were now more ministers available than there had been earlier, and the pastorate of Unity Church was undoubtedly a more desirable position than it had been before Gannett and Crothers had enriched it.

This latest minister-less period lasted from February 1894 until February 1895, when the most promising of the available ministers, William R. Lord, of Boston, was duly installed at Unity Church.

A graduate of Amherst College, Lord attended Union Theological Seminary and, like Crothers, was ordained a Presbyterian minister. Also, like his predecessor, he later rejected his Presbyterian training and beliefs when he found himself more in accord with Unitarian thought. When he received the call to St. Paul he was the pastor of the Harrison Square Unitarian Church in Dorchester, a suburb of Boston. While there he had been zealously interested in public affairs and had become one of the officers of the Massachusetts Reform Club.

Lord's installation at Unity Church was noteworthy for the presence not only of Crothers, who had come from Cambridge to deliver the sermon, but of Dr. Edward P. Ingersoll, pastor of the Park Congregational Church, Dr. Alexander N. Carson, pastor of the Central Presbyterian Church, and Dr. C. B. Wilcox, pastor of the First Methodist Episcopal Church, all of St. Paul. Dr. Ingersoll even took part in the service, delivering an address to the new minister and his congregation. Apparently, in widening circles, Unitarianism was being accepted as a legitimate denomination.

Among the activities within the church, there were a few new developments. Lord himself took over the job of superintendent of the Sunday school, with R. S. Mackintosh as his assistant. In 1894-95 the formerly thriving Unity Club (now outgrown by the older people, we are told) was replaced by a study club. Under the tutelage of the minister, the earnest members of this group read and discussed innumerable literary and cultural works. In place of the old Unity Club another organization, the Young People's Guild, was established.

In January of 1896, through the instrumentality of Lord, Booker T. Washington of the Tuskegee Normal and Industrial Institute lectured at the People's Church in St. Paul on the work that he was doing with black men at the institute. The following day he met with the women of Unity Church. This was of particular interest to them because for the two previous years they had contributed financially to the institute, besides assisting in the support of the Post Office Mission. Now, in 1897, the members of this long-established group voted to merge with the National Alliance of Unitarian Women, and in this form continued to give assistance to the church, as they had already done for so many years. There are abundant instances of their industry and helpfulness, as, for example in 1905, when their donation of $300 cleared the church of its remaining debt. Not until approximately sixty years later did the Alliance give up its independence to join the larger and younger Minister's Guild.

It was about this time, too, that a second Beals daughter replaced her sister as church organist. From 1896 to 1921 Mrs. Caroline Beals Jilson held this essential post, rounding out twenty-five years of service to the church. After Mrs. Jilson's death in 1947, her daughter, Eleanor, presented a plaque to Unity Church in memory of her parents, the Frank B. Jilsons.

The designer of this memorial was Mrs. Marian Greene Barney, a lifelong and close friend of the donor.

Unfortunately, Lord's pastorate, despite its auspicious beginning, was short-lived. There is little specific information available about his ministry, but comments from contemporary church members imply that he did not particularly inspire his congregation. Equally unfortunate is the fact that we know so little about why he left. In tendering his resignation on October 3, 1897, Lord gave as his reasons only the following:

> I have come to the conclusion that the welfare of Unity Church and the good of the liberal cause in St. Paul, will be served by my withdrawal from the position of your minister.
>
> St. Paul has but one liberal church, and that church should be strong. In it all the liberal elements of the city ought to be unified. And it should also attract many now outside of all churches. It is clear to me that I am not the man to bring about these results.... There are other fields in which I believe I can do better work than I am doing here."[51]

Once again the pattern for replacing a minister had to be repeated. Lord preached two more sermons. Then the pulpit was filled each Sunday by substitute speakers. Happily, Crothers returned to St. Paul for a four-day visit to old friends, preached a sermon on December 9, and was given a reception in the church parlor afterwards. Noted Kelley in his chronicle, "Happiness was shown in the expression of every face."[52]

It was not until October 7, 1898, that a call was finally extended to Clarence Leslie Diven of Southington, Connecticut, who had been one of the September interim preachers and who had been highly recommended by the American Unitarian Association. He accepted the call, asking only that his installation services take place during the sessions of the

---

[51] William R. Lord to the officers and members of Unity Church, October 3, 1897, in Kelley Journal, p. 203.
[52] Kelley Journal, p.206.

Minnesota Unitarian Conference. The conference was to be held in Unity Church on November 2, and Crothers was to be present.

Diven was forty-four years old when he came to Unity Church. He was born in Winchester, Kentucky, but aside from a quite remarkable record of scholarship, we have little information about him. He was graduated from the University of Missouri with highest honors in 1880, studied for the ministry at Union Theological Seminary and Harvard Divinity School, then continued his education in Europe. After serving several Congregational pastorates he returned to Boston to resume his theological studies there. At this time he adopted Unitarianism and just prior to coming to St. Paul he received his doctor's degree from the Chicago Theological Seminary.

As Diven settled into his new ministry he had good prospects of a successful future. But far too soon for his particular qualities to make any mark on the church or community, he became critically ill, and only a few days later he died from peritonitis on January 18, 1900.

Unfortunately there are no available records of Diven's accomplishments. The article written for the *St. Paul Pioneer Press* at the time of his death says of him, "Few of the Northwestern clergy have had the advantage of a culture so thorough. ... The city loses a man esteemed for active Christianity, admired for his scholarship and eloquence."[53] In spite of this high praise for his intellectual achievements, the impression Diven has left in the minds of his parishioners is that of a likeable personality but not a stimulating minister. Since he was hardly granted time in his brief fifteen months in St. Paul to demonstrate his abilities, it is apparent that his congregation also had too little time to judge his true potential.

---

[53] St. Paul Pioneer Press, January 19, 1900.

Figure 12
Three 19th Century Ministers

Clay MacCauley, 1884–1886
Minnesota Historical Society

William R. Lord, 1895-1897
Minnesota Historical Society

Clarence L. Diven, 1898-1900
Courtesy of the Unitarian
Universalist World

IV. New Church on the Hill 1900-1917

Diven was replaced, fortunately, with more dispatch than had been usual in the past. In early June, 1900, after an interval of only five months, Richard Wilson Boynton, from the Unitarian Church in Roslindale, Massachusetts, came to St. Paul to preach two sermons. The congregation, being favorably impressed, gave its unanimous approval of him as its new minister. A call was telegraphed to Boynton, and his acceptance was prompt. It was arranged that his pastorate would start in the fall. Boynton had served a very popular five-year ministry at the smaller church and leaving his congregation was difficult, but his former members graciously sent a congratulatory letter to be read as part of Boynton's installation ceremony.

This service took place on October 2, 1900. Crothers, much of whose affection must still have remained with his former congregation in St. Paul, came from Cambridge to deliver the sermon. The clergy of the Twin Cities were represented by Henry M. Simmons, the long-time minister of the First Unitarian Society of Minneapolis, and by Alexander McGregor, pastor of Park Congregational Church in St. Paul.

Another New Englander, Boynton was born in Dorchester, Massachusetts, in 1870. He was a graduate of Meadville Theological School and Harvard Divinity School, subsequently receiving his ordination at the Roslindale church in 1895. He is remembered as a rather small, dark-haired man, neat in appearance and precise in manner. Though seemingly colorless in some ways, he held very firm opinions. He was an excellent parish minister, though not an outstanding preacher. His views were liberal for those days and in one instance he provoked a woman member, Mrs. R. A. Greene, into stalking out of church in the middle of his sermon. She objected to Boynton's stated approval of Theodore Roosevelt's "Trust Busting." This action by the distinguished-looking woman caused a mild sensation, especially because she occupied a seat in one of the front pews (in the days when each family pre-empted and held its own

Figure 13 Richard W. Boynton
Minister of Unity Church, 1900-1907
Minnesota Historical Society

particular pew throughout a lifetime) and made her "protest" march the entire length of the center aisle of the church.

But Boynton also possessed a gentleness that endeared him to his parishioners. It was his habit to address some small personal remark to each new member as he or she joined the church.

On the other hand, Boynton once spoke of the danger of the Unitarian services becoming purely intellectual and in consequence not appealing to the young people. He also felt his own personality was partially responsible for their lack of interest. Therefore he advocated enriching the service by introducing something of an emotional element.

Two months before Boynton's arrival, the death of the long-standing member and faithful diarist of Unity Church, William H. Kelley, had saddened the congregation. As a fitting memorial to him, a special meeting of Unity Church was held in April 1900, for the purpose of adopting the resolution quoted here in part:

> The church owes him gratitude for many valuable services, both as a church officer and as the historian of the church, the latter duty voluntarily assumed and assiduously performed. ... As a citizen he was public-spirited ... and in private business he discharged a trust of great importance with intelligence and fidelity.[54]

Fortunately for Unity Church, Miss Emma Kelley, with the assistance of Mrs. F. B. Tiffany and Miss Delia Cheney, carried on the diary without interruption. But without Kelley's colorful touch and careful detail regarding people and events, the record now becomes less picturesque.

In 1901 the congregation was introduced to an interesting innovation. On Easter Sunday twenty-three persons formally joined the church in the simple ceremony, inaugurated by Boynton, that still prevails with little change today.

By early 1902 the parishioners and the minister were already planning the celebration of the church's thirtieth anniversary. It was held on February 28. Emma Kelley, who had inherited her father's interest in the weather that accompanied events, recorded that although the evening was wet and snowy, one hundred and ninety persons made their way to the church. And

---

[54] Kelley Journal, p.227. Kelley was employed by the Frist National Bank of St. Paul as a bookkeeper.

Crothers once again loyally came from Cambridge for the occasion.

Apparently, the passing of the church's thirtieth anniversary stimulated the aspirations of its members. For, shortly afterward, the congregation began talking about a new building. The inside of the "church home" so thought fully planned twenty-two years before was still functionally adequate. But changes were taking place in the Wabasha Street area that made the location less than desirable. The neighborhood was deteriorating. It had become noisy with street-cars, and dirty. Many years later Boynton, reminiscing to Frederick Eliot, added a humorous touch concerning one of the trials encountered in the degenerating area. "I wonder," he wrote, "how many recall when the preacher's voice was liable at any moment to be hopelessly drowned by the penetrating voice of the laundryman's donkey in the yard just in back of the church."[55] For these reasons many downtown residents had moved up on the hill and some of their churches were following them.

At a trustees' meeting in March 1902, the matter of a new building was first discussed seriously. Benjamin Sommers, Charles W. Ames, and E. H. Bailey were appointed to a Real Estate Committee. As the investigation of possible sites progressed, five more members were added: Francis B. Tiffany, Thomas Gannett Holyoke (the architect), and three women, Mrs. Ames, Mrs. Bailey, and Mrs. Tiffany.

On April 2 a special meeting of the congregation unanimously approved the securing of a new building site. To save time and to take advantage of an opportunity to buy the lots on favorable terms, Ames, Sommers, and C. H. Kellogg agreed to underwrite and purchase, on their own responsibility, the three lots at the corner of Portland and Grotto Streets. The cost involved was $3,700, including taxes. Later the lots were to be transferred to the Unity Church Corporation.

---

[55] Richard W. Boynton To Frederick M. Eliot, February 1, 1921, on the dedication of the Parish Hall.

Now the matter of a new church "up on the hill" was gathering enough momentum to warrant asking Holyoke to present some plans. By January of 1905 Ames was able to report that the subscriptions had reached $10,000. He also personally guaranteed a loan of $10,000 on the Wabasha Street property.

With $20,000 thus available, and with Holyoke's blue prints of a church that looked like a church eminently satisfactory, even to those who had rejoiced in their Queen Anne cottage, a contract for the new building was let to F. J. Romer and Sons. This time the contractor was well financed and reliable, the subsoil of the lots was solid, and an interested architect who was also a member of the church was constantly on hand to supervise construction.

Holyoke had presented two plans; the first consisted of a parish hall, a sanctuary to seat about three hundred persons, and a connecting tower. The second plan omitted the tower and substituted for it a less costly enclosed vestibule which could be replaced when funds permitted. The first plan was adopted, since the Ames loan made erection of the tower possible, but a parish hall had to be excluded because of the additional cost. The building, Norman-Romanesque in style, was to be constructed of a local yellow limestone, with trim of Bedford stone. The total cost, including heating plant and gas fixtures, came to approximately $34,000.

On the interior of the church, huge red cedar beams arched over the sanctuary, and leaded glass windows lined the outside aisles. (These windows came to be considered by younger people as lacking in aesthetic value, and as they deteriorated with the years were the cause of frequent de bates on whether to replace or repair them. This dilemma was solved when they were destroyed by fire in 1963.) A shallow but high alcove, also arched, was cut into the back wall of the chancel behind the altar. And to the right of the altar was space for the choir and the organ. (No record of the type of organ installed has been found.) The corresponding space at the left led to the church parlor. The pews were of light-colored oak, and the first memorial gift to the new building was oak pulpit furniture, purchased with the proceeds of A. H. Wimbish's estate. (This was later donated to the Hanska church.) An amusing Victorian addendum appears in the minutes of the April 5, 1908, meeting of the Board of Trustees where it is stated that "Mrs. Ames reported the need of a bench in the tower vestibule for fainting ladies."

Figure 14 Laying cornerstones of Unity Church
Minnesota Historical Society

The dirt started flying on April 1, 1905, as soon as the frost was out of the ground. At the ground-breaking festival, Boynton's daughter, Mary, turned the first shovelful of sod, and Ames's youngest son, Theodore, turned the second, after which all the other children joined in the digging. The congregation today may contain at least one child who can recall that occasion. By June it was time to lay the cornerstone. To the congregation's delight, Gannett, with his wife and daughter, had come from Rochester, New York, to be present at the ceremony, "linking very significantly," says Emma Kelley, "the old with the New." His address, planned as the main feature of the service, was cut short by a severe shower, but was continued that evening in the old church he had been instrumental in building.

Less than a year had elapsed from the groundbreaking of the new church to its completion when, on December 3, 1905, the final service was held in the old building on Wabasha. In his last sermon there, Boynton said:

> These walls that have echoed to our songs and our petitions we leave behind, with thoughts of the blessings and the peace that have come to us here. ... May that same spirit of unity go with us. You, the people, have been the real Unity Church and are so still.[56]

Figure 15 Unity Church, 1905
Minnesota Historical Society

---

[56] Kelley Journal, p. 253.

The dedication of the new church was held December 10, 1905. Crothers was again present to deliver an address, after which the congregation joined in reading one of Gannett's responsive services and the ceremony closed with a hymn written by Charles Gordon Ames, father of Charles W. Ames.

It had been hoped that the now empty building on Wabasha might be quickly and advantageously sold, but no one seemed to want it. It grew dingier month by month as its neighborhood grew noisier and dirtier. Eventually the St. Paul Turnverein felt that without the pews and pulpit it would serve nicely for a gymnasium, and bought it for $14,000. This was considerably less than the original cost, but the people of Unity Church had undoubtedly been compensated for the $10,000 difference in the satisfying years in their first church. (In 1943 the Wabasha Street building was destroyed by fire.)

Figure 16 Women's Group, Unity Church Circa 1908
Minnesota Historical Society

In February 1907, Boynton, who had been unwell for some time, asked the Board of Trustees for a six-months' leave of absence. His intention was to spend the time abroad in rest and study. Thoughtfully he had arranged for his temporary replacement by Francis Tiffany of Cambridge, who came to St. Paul in May. In October Boynton returned, but the following month his health again became uncertain and he was compelled to try a milder climate. Regretfully he tendered his resignation, regretfully his congregation accepted it, and the new church "up on the hill" was again without a minister.

On leaving Unity Church, Boynton was invited to teach at the University of Buffalo. He became a professor of philosophy there and remained as emeritus from 1937-57. During these twenty years he also had some Unitarian pastorates and did some writing, receiving recognition for one book in particular entitled *Beyond Mythology*. In spite of his earlier ill-health Boynton lived to be ninety-one. He died in Florida on November 30, 1961.

Boynton's successor was John Dumont Reid, minister of the Unitarian Church in Greenfield, Massachusetts. He agreed to begin his pastoral duties on March 1 at a salary of $3,000.

The ninth minister of Unity Church, Reid was born in 1861 in Vevay, Indiana, into a cultured family. His grandmother, Julia Dumont, was a teacher and a well-known literary figure in Indiana. His father was a Presbyterian minister. Reid was educated at Wabash College and Yale University Divinity School. To help defray his college expenses he did some teaching and for a time worked at Marshall Field and Company in Chicago, after which he served Congregational parishes in Sheboygan, Wisconsin, Fergus Falls, Minnesota, and Great Falls, Montana. While at this latter post he made the difficult transition to a more liberal religion, accepting the pastorate of the Unitarian church in the same city, At his next church in Greenfield he was ordained a Unitarian minister.

In St. Paul the new minister, his wife, and four children lived on Holly Avenue, which church members had begun to call

Figure 17 John D. Reid
Minister of Unity Church, 1908-1917
Courtesy of All Souls Unitarian Church, Greenfield, Massachusetts

"Unitarian Row" since this street was also inhabited by the Beals, the Greenes, the Putnams, the Sawyers, and the Baileys.

Reid's nine-year pastorate was successful in some areas and disappointing in others. The problem seemed to lie in the temperament of Reid himself, who, according to a biographical essay by John Malick, written for the June 27, 1929, issue of the Christian Register, was a minister of the older, and vanishing, tradition of the prophet-philosopher, to whom the increasing demands of parish administration were uncongenial. He was a quiet, retiring man, with a pleasant personality, and an interesting talker in private conversation. But he did not mix well with groups of people nor initiate activities, and evidently the best of his qualities were not apparent in his sermons or in his dealings with the congregation.

The results of Reid's deficiencies were a severe falling off of the membership in the church and of attendance in the Sunday school. The minutes of the Board of Trustees from 1910-1914 show that unusual attempts were being made to find new financial contributors to the church. And F. O. Willius, superintendent of the Sunday school in 1910, repeatedly pleaded with church members to encourage their children to attend classes, the total enrollment of which had fallen well below one hundred. By 1916 the congregation was restive over the situation and we find the following in the May minutes of the Board of Trustees:

> For some time, it has been known to the Trustees that a considerable portion of members of Unity Church desire a change in the pastorate. It has also been stated that the minister, Rev. John D. Reid, desires to secure a pulpit in New England or the East.

The situation was resolved by Reid's resignation in early 1917. Unity Church was his last regular pastorate, and after leaving St. Paul, he served almost entirely in interim positions. He died in Salem, Massachusetts, in 1929.

Unity Church fortunately could again rely upon its energetic parishioners to carry on the church programs; and some innovations were instituted. The women of the church had maintained their active Alliance and in addition had contributed in many varied capacities, including raising money and helping to staff the Sunday school. Now, in 1914, they organized a Junior Alliance, composed of the younger church women, to supplement their work. Mrs. F. B. Tiffany was the originator and Miss Elizabeth Ames (Mrs. Norris Jackson) the president of this group. Later, under Frederick Eliot, the Junior Alliance broke away from the older branch and undertook projects to assist the minister (the very first of which was to purchase a new robe for him).

One highly successful organization which was formed at Reid's suggestion was the Men's Club. At a dinner furnished by the church women, plans for it were discussed, and by October 1912, it came into actual existence with an Executive Committee consisting of Reid, F. B. Tiffany, Henry Randall, William Laidlaw, and Charles L. Sommers. This informal group held five meetings each season. At each meeting a specific subject was presented by an assigned member or guest speaker, followed by general discussion. Participation was not confined to men of the church and there were a number of outside members. The principal officer was the secretary, a post filled initially by Tiffany and secondly by Sommers. The dinners continued to be supplied by the women. In 1919 the Men's Club was succeeded by the Unity Church chapter of the Laymen's League—a national Unitarian organization.

When F. O. Willius resigned as superintendent of the Sunday school, that position was filled by Miss Clara Sommers (Mrs. Henry Randall). Working with her was a committee including Reid, one member from the Women's Alliance, and one member from the Board of Trustees. Walter Chapin remembers that Miss Sommers was actually managing the Sunday school and doing an excellent job of it. Between 1914-18 the superintendent's post was held by Edward B. Young, who also at one time or another was treasurer of the Laymen's League and a member of the Board of Trustees and of the committee for the church-sponsored Boy Scout troop. Contemporary members of the church have all mentioned the dedication and excellence of the Sunday school teachers of those years and the lasting impression they made on their pupils. Under this fine management class attendance again began to increase.

Figure 18 Group of members in front of Unity Church
Approximately 1915. Minnesota Historical Society

Figure 19 The sanctuary prior to 1925
Minnesota Historical Society

When World War I began in August 1914, the church women found time to take on another activity, American Aid for French Wounded. With the entrance of the United States into the war in 1917, they organized the Unity Church Auxiliary of the St. Paul Chapter of the Red Cross and devoted their meetings to making surgical dressings and hospital garments.

In this same year, on December 22, Joseph S. Sewall died at the age of ninety-one. He was the last of that earliest group of "misguided unbelievers" who had contributed "to sustain Unitarian preaching in St. Paul." This year also seems to mark the end of the early development of Unity Church, to be followed by a period of rapid growth and change that was a part of the changing times.

V. The Prosperous Years; Frederick May Eliot
1917-1937

Fortunately a candidate for the pulpit was almost immediately available, and just as fortunately, that candidate had been groomed for the ministry by Unity's friend and former minister, Dr. Crothers.

The congregation's choice was Frederick May Eliot of Cambridge, Massachusetts. He preached his first sermon in St. Paul in late January, 1917. Emma Kelley jotted down in the journal, with what was to set a record for understatement, "His sermon and personality made a strong impression on the congregation, in fact that impression is likely to be a lasting one."[57]

When Unity Church issued an invitation to Eliot, he accepted it with the understanding that he would shortly be called into service as chaplain of the Massachusetts General Hospital Unit. He had time, before he reported for duty, to return to St. Paul, deliver his first regular sermon on September 17, and to be duly installed on October 11. The installation was made doubly impressive by the presence not only of Crothers but also of Frederick Eliot's father, Christopher Rhodes Eliot, minister of Bullfinch Place Church in Boston, who delivered to his son "the charge to the pastor."

The expected mobilization came in 1918 and Chaplain Eliot sailed for France in August. His station was American Base Hospital #7, located at Tours.

During the fall and winter of that year the flu epidemic that was sweeping the country led to the closing of Unity Church on Sundays. Services were not resumed until January 1919. The pulpit was then filled by visiting ministers, when available, and by university professors. When the war ended, Eliot returned

---

[57] Kelley Journal, p. 284.

Figure 20 Frederick May Eliot
Minnesota Historical Society

from his army duty, and, beginning in April 1919, settled
purpose fully into his ministry.

Frederick May Eliot was to be the minister of Unity Church for
twenty years. Born in 1889, he was the second of our ministers
to be a Unitarian by birth. He had a distinguished background.
He was the great-grandson of the man who helped to establish
All Souls Unitarian Church in Washington, D.C. in 1821; and
the grandson, son, and nephew of Unitarian ministers. His
mother was also a Unitarian. His grandfather was the founder
of Washington University in St. Louis; his father, named for
Christopher Rhodes (an incorporator of Washington

University) was a graduate of that university and of Harvard Divinity School.

Eliot's education was received at Harvard College, from which he was graduated summa cum laude with a degree in government. While still an undergraduate, he had attended Crothers' First Parish Church in Cambridge, Massachusetts, and it was in part due to Crothers' influence that Eliot decided to enter Harvard Divinity School. After his ordination in 1915, he served as Crothers' assistant. He married Elizabeth Berkeley Lee from Brunswick, Maine, and they had two sons.

On his arrival in St. Paul in 1917, Eliot was only twenty-eight years old, but his parishioners soon learned to know him as a dynamic, self-confident young man. He had great charm, but could, on occasion, display a quick temper and a stubborn desire to carry out his projects in his own way. His tremendous vitality made him not only an outstanding minister but a leader in the community as well. In his biographical essay on Eliot, Clinton Lee Scott gave this description of him:

> His was a well-balanced ministry. He was a forceful figure in the pulpit, with his tall, manly frame, strong features ... rich pleasing voice—altogether a well-constructed trumpet for prayer and song.... Parish work was fitted to the needs of the people. He knew his parishioners in their homes and they grew to rely upon his counsel and to trust his confidence.[58]

Under this vital leadership many innovations took place at Grotto and Portland, not merely in the pulpit but in all church activities. In the first place Eliot preferred more ceremony and emotional content in the service than had been customary before him. Consequently, the Sunday service, which had been almost Quaker-simple, now became more elaborate. Candles and flowers were used on the altar, which the congregation, following its minister's example, was no longer reluctant to call an altar. Music became a more important adjunct to the service.

---

[58] Clinton Lee Scott, These Live Tomorrow: Twenty Unitarian-Universalist Biographies (Boston, 1964), p. 272.

Aside from the addition of a quartet in 1906 and a renovation of the organ in 1915, little change had been made in the area of church music prior to Eliot's ministry. In 1921 Mrs. Caroline Beals Jilson terminated her twenty-five years as church organist. She was replaced briefly by Chandler Goldthwaite and then by William P. Dunn, who also held a professorship at the University of Minnesota. At about the same time a choir was established under the direction of the leading soprano, Miss Harriet Cassidy, and the results were a team of competent musicians and excellent music. For a short period in 1926, an accomplished soloist, Mrs. Agnes Rast Snyder, replaced the choir. Two years later a chorus of eight voices, in addition to Mrs. Snyder, who doubled as director and soloist, was reinstated. When Dunn was forced to resign in 1928, because of ill-health, Unity Church had the good fortune to obtain the services of Miss Virginia Wetherbee (later to become Mrs. Louis Powell) who has to this day in 1971 been instrumental in offering fine musicianship to the congregation. By 1925 the old organ was removed to make room for a new Skinner organ, generously given by the Cochran family in memory of their mother, Mrs. Emilie B. Cochran. This instrument remained in use until destroyed by fire in 1963.

Religious education was also of tremendous interest to Eliot, and here, too, he introduced new and positive ideas. Preferring to be in charge of his own projects, he undertook the conducting of the church school services and the supervision of the programs himself with a committee assisting him. Part of his plan was to grade the classes more carefully and to adjust the lessons more closely to the age groups of the children. On certain Sundays the pupils were invited into the church proper to hear the opening portion of the adult service. Following a brief talk by Eliot, geared to the children's level, the young people returned to their classrooms. Eliot's concern with the Sunday school showed results, since on his arrival the number of children enrolled was thirty-five, by 1923 that number had doubled, and by 1931 the total had increased to nearly two hundred.

Figure 21 Girls conducting experiment in science class
Unity Church, St. Paul. Appr. 1930.
Minnesota Historical Society

Figure 22 Ruth Stevens' science class
Unity Church, St. Paul. Appr. 1930.
Minnesota Historical Society

Other innovations stemmed from the new minister's love of the dramatic, even the symbolic, as demonstrated by the introduction of pageants into the Sunday school curriculum. At Easter the pupils performed "The Sacred Flame, or the Red Cross Knight." In this drama, adapted from a story by Selma Lagerlof, the flame, passed on from generation to generation by the faithfulness of men, symbolized the immortality of the spiritual life. Except for two other experiments in Easter drama, this play was given every year until 1934. Miss Beulah Brown will be remembered by the young people of that period for her excellent directing of these popular (though not typically Unitarian) productions.

Figure 23 Easter pageant, Unity Church, St. Paul. 1920
Minnesota Historical Society

In 1920 Mrs. George Morgan was asked to head a committee to further dramatize church school services, and was largely responsible for beginning the tradition of the Christmas pageant, still presented much as it was then. Being a part of the pageant cast has, from the very first, been regarded as a special privilege. The idea of placing gifts near the manger as a concrete expression of the Christmas spirit of giving had its inception in the close contact between Miss Constance Currie, director of the Neighborhood House, and Unity Church. After the pageant the presents were distributed among the children living in the Neighborhood House area.

With spring each year came another annual treat, the Sunday school picnic. An old tradition now, the earlier outings were sometimes held in Minnehaha Park, where, according to Walter L. Chapin, Jr., the picnickers arrived by bus or boat from downtown St. Paul. For several years the White Bear Lake home of Mr. and Mrs. William West, Sr., offered a very pleasant site for the picnics, and for about ten years Mr. and Mrs. Henry Sommers opened their Hudson, Wisconsin, summer place for the event. In 1925 the annual affair took an original turn because the church members wished to raise money for the new kindergarten room, to be a surprise for Eliot on his return from a leave of absence. Mrs. Sommers has described the pony rides (necessarily short since there was only one small and ornery pony), the museums, the games of horseshoe, fifteen-minute turns at tennis, and other attractions, each available for five or ten cents. Even the viewing of her mother's beautiful garden involved a small fee, a fact which offended Mrs. Henry C. James until she was appeased by being allowed to serve free punch. Beginning with 1941 the church picnic site was transferred to Lake Carver, at the Neighborhood House camp, where the picnics continue to be held today.

Meanwhile the urge for growth in the church structure itself was building up. Eliot had found the Sunday school classrooms dingy and inadequate and there had been talk for some time of constructing the parish house wing which had been included in the original plans. At this time Magnus Jemne, who had entered Holyoke's firm after the war, began to assume the role of architect for Unity Church's projects. He continued to do so for many years. Jemne became prominent in his field and a member of the church he so ably served.

A dinner and business meeting was arranged for January 31, 1920, and one hundred persons were present. Charles L. Sommers, chairman of the Building Committee, was ready with plans and cost figures. The new addition, designed by the architectural firm of Holyoke, Jemne, and Davis, was to include a dining room, kitchen, and classrooms in the basement, an auditorium and stage on the first floor, and a chapel above the auditorium. When presented with the cost of the project, the congregation realized fully what postwar inflation was doing to the economy. To complete the entire addition would cost considerably more than had the original church itself. It was voted to compromise by temporarily leaving the space for the chapel unfinished. The members responded generously to a second solicitation and Sommers and his committee were authorized to go ahead with the plans.

Figure 24 Unity Church after addition of the parish hall (1920)
Minnesota Historical Society

By early fall, the wing was completed, and almost immediately put to good use, since many organizations desired to rent space in it. Among these were a dancing school, the Summit School kindergarten, the Blind Association, a Boy Scout troop, and a pre-school group. The final cost was $41,000, of which $18,000 had to be borrowed.

The new ell had now taken up all the surface space available. But by 1929 more room was already needed for the growing Sunday school. The only piece of ground left for enlargement was the remainder of the basement. When that project was completed in 1930 the entire area under the original building had been excavated and made usable.

Figure 25 The sanctuary between 1925 and 1964
Minnesota Historical Society

On April 3, 1921, the church lost one of its dynamic and most generous members with the death of Charles W. Ames at the age of sixty-six. He had served staunchly through several pastorates and the gaps in between, and his loss was deeply felt. In 1923 the members of the church acknowledged their debt to him and their appreciation of all he had done by dedicating the Ames chapel to his memory.

Figure 26 Mr. and Mrs. Charles W. Ames, about 1910
From a photograph owned by Mr. and Mrs. Norris Jackson

Again the people of the congregation gave generously to help furnish this lovely room, designed primarily for the morning service of the Sunday school. The stained glass windows at the back of the chapel, the work of Charles J. Connick of Boston, were the gift of the Informal Club, an organization entirely apart from the church, but founded by Ames. Woven into the background design of the windows, which tell the story of St. Martin, are a tablet of the Commandments, showing Ames's vocation, the publishing of law books, and the arms of the French Republic, representing his sincere admiration of the French nation's courage during the first World War.

Figure 27 The Charles W. Ames Chapel, about 1950
Minnesota Historical Society

Many of the furnishings in the chapel, including the altar, chairs (no longer there), tall candlesticks, and bronze angels, were the gifts of Mrs. George Metcalf. The collection plates were given by Mrs. J. P. MacLaren in memory of her mother, Mrs. Churchill Gersting. The lectern, the first gift for the new chapel, was carved by Olaf Carlquist and given by Unity Guild. The chapel organ also was a gift, donated by members of the Sommers family as a memorial to their parents, Mr. and Mrs. George S. Sommers. (This organ has recently been replaced by a new one.) The bell with St. George and the dragon, a replica of early Italian ironwork, was given by C. L. Ames, and the bronze statue, "The Appeal to the Great Spirit," was a special memorial gift.

The death of the original architect, Holyoke, in 1925, was a second great loss to the church and the community. In recognition of his lasting contributions, the Board of Trustees adopted a resolution which read in part: "As William Channing Gannett was the architect of the Church Spiritual, Thomas Gannett Holyoke was the architect of the bodily church. ... It stands today as a monument to him."

Church organizations were also undergoing change at this time as Eliot tried to meet the needs of his parish. Greater stress was laid on the activities of the young people, and for their benefit three new groups were founded:

> 1919—Unity Guild (predecessor of Tower Club): part of the National Young People's Union. The purpose of this organization was to prepare its youth for membership in the church. The program, in addition to social events, consisted of studies of all aspects of the church, its history, administration, and philosophies. There were eight charter members: Helen and Doris Cushman, Dorothy Sommers, Frances West, Walter Chapin, Jr., Davidson Sommers, Lydia Buckley, and Ferdinand Fetter.

> 1925— Ulysses Club (ages 17-25): also part of a national Unitarian organization. This group was very active, participating in discussions, projects to assist the church, and social affairs, including numerous amateur dramatics under the direction of Miss Beulah Brown.

> 1930—Tower Club (senior high school): a very popular program still in existence today. A Sunday evening candlelight service was followed by supper and discussion. Those church members who were of high-school age during Eliot's ministry will remember how the club received its name. Originally the meetings were held in the tower under the church spire, until the narrow stairs winding up to the room became unsafe and the room itself too dingy and cramped for use.

The Business and Professional Women's Club, established in 1935, set itself some specific goals: to help small Unitarian churches in the state; to help the minister; and to give assistance or sponsorship to local social agencies, such as Neighborhood House. These women also have taken upon themselves the responsibility of serving many of the church dinners. The first board consisted of Mrs. Frances Locke, Miss Mary Chapin, and Miss Josephine Downey. In 1941 the members renamed their group the Elizabeth Eliot Club in honor of Mrs. Eliot, and as such it exists today.

All of this building, organizing, and expansion attested to the vitality of Eliot's ministry and the capability of the minister himself. But, as was the case with his predecessors, Eliot had behind him competent and hardworking people of the church as well as staff members.

Gradually, through the last decade, the older generation of the Ameses, the Tiffanys, the Baileys, the Chapins, were yielding their places to a younger group. Some of these men and women were children, even grandchildren of the original or very early membership. Up to this time the attendance lists of the Sunday school, for instance, showed a preponderance of children named Ames, Sommers, Turner, West, Chapin, Tiffany, Cushman, etc. But more and more Unity Church's liberal viewpoint was attracting the native St. Paulites, who were not necessarily from the New England background of so many of the pioneer Unitarians.

With the growth in membership and activities, the church found it necessary to furnish the minister with a paid staff. Between 1923 and 1926 the position of parish assistant was held successively by Miss Helen Kimberley and Miss Ruth Kolling. In 1926 Newton E. Lincoln, formerly Midwestern secretary of the Unitarian Laymen's League, was hired as executive secretary to take charge of the office and to relieve Eliot of administrative details. Lincoln kept this position until 1929, when he was succeeded by Elizabeth Buckley. For the following ten years Miss Buckley was Eliot's invaluable assistant, and, when she left Unity Church in 1939, she did so in order to continue working for him in his post as president of the American Unitarian Association in Boston.

The number of those contributing financially to the church had, by 1926, increased, from the 1921 figure of one hundred and twenty-seven, to a total of almost two hundred. At this time the minister's salary was set at $6,000 (the parish house at 807 Fairmount, like the other former parsonages, was rented for the minister and the utilities paid), and the annual budget at around $15,000.

These were the prosperous years of the nineteen-twenties, which Eliot spoke of as the years of generous giving, because of the numerous gifts, memorials, and bequests made to the church. Those known to the writer (in addition to the gifts for the Ames Chapel) are listed here.

Memorials and Gifts
1. To Captain Norman Claussen, only member of the church to die in action during World War I: a bronze tablet designed by Magnus Jemne; gift of Battery B of St. Paul, dedicated in 1925. Ames Chapel.[59]
2. To William Channing Gannett: a bronze plaque inscribed with a verse from Gannett's hymn, "Here Be No Man a Stranger"; gift of Mrs. Charles H. Clark, 1929. Foyer, south wall.
3. To Thomas Gannett Holyoke: a memorial tablet designed by Magnus Jemne; gift of Holyoke's sister, Mrs. William Davis, 1925. Foyer, east wall.
4. To Mrs. Emilie B. Cochran: the Skinner Organ; gift of her children, 1924. Burned in 1963 fire.
5. To Mrs. E. H. Bailey: church altar table; gift of E. H. Bailey, 1930.
6. To Samuel McChord Crothers: a memorial tablet designed by Magnus Jemne; bas-relief portrait modeled by Henry K. Bush Brown; gift of the members of the church, 1929. Foyer, south wall.
7. To Edward Blake Young: a bronze tablet designed by Magnus Jemne, in recognition of Young's work with

---

[59] Correction: Norman F. Claussen received the Silver Star for "gallantry in action" and for "brilliant leadership" during his tour. In October 1918, shortly after returning to the United States, he died of influenza. Source: MNHS

young people and his years of service to the church; gift of Mrs. Young, 1929. Foyer, east wall.

8. Collection plates, carved by Olaf C. Carlquist; gift of the Ulysses Club.
9. Altar candlesticks; gift of Mrs. Charles Bunn. Burned in 1963 fire.

Now that the church possessed a new organ it seemed appropriate to add a final aesthetic touch. Until 1925 the congregation had faced bare walls, exposed organ pipes, and a choir prominently seated in front of the pews. Therefore, Jemne was commissioned to design partitions which would conceal the pipes and the choir, and simultaneously enrich the sanctuary. To accomplish this an enclosure was built at either side of the pulpit platform and screened in with oak panels, intricately hand carved into leaf and flower tracery by the craftsman, Olaf Carlquist. A similarly decorated panel, extending several feet above the altar, was added to the wall at the back of the arched alcove. The much-admired heads on the extensions of the red cedar beams were also added at that time. All of this handsomely executed woodwork was consumed in the 1963 fire.[60]

Despite Unity Church's much increased membership the social side of church life continued to play an important role. The annual dinners were almost always gala affairs. A popular form of entertainment at this time was the costume party, one of which, held in November 1927, was a particularly memorable occasion. The central theme was the Victorian era. Mrs. Benjamin Sommers, being of the proper size and shape, was prevailed upon to represent the Queen herself, and, according to contemporary reports, was the "living reincarnation of the English monarch." Miss Hester Pollock made a fine John Brown (Victoria's faithful attendant); Harvey B. Fuller enacted the role of Disraeli; and the church bulletin of that month tells us that "Messrs. Baird, Forbes, Laidlaw, and C. L. Sommers formed

---

[60]Note: Several of the heads were discovered to have survived and are on display at Unity Church.

a quartet of Czechoslovakian chefs that would suitably grace any royal kitchen."

In the meantime, on February 25, 1922, the church had noted its fiftieth anniversary. Though Eliot delivered special sermons at morning and vesper services, the true celebration was postponed until May 6, when it was possible for both Crothers and Boynton to participate as the principal dinner speakers. Several of the older members were called upon to present historical sketches and reminiscences of the first and vital fifty years of the church. And the evening was climaxed with a touch of the contemporary era when the congregation bestowed upon the minister a new Ford automobile.

The following year the church received a first warning that it was in danger of losing its widely admired minister. A call came to Eliot from the First Unitarian Church of Chicago. The Board of Trustees immediately appointed a committee consisting of Charles Sommers, Miss Anita Furness, George Morgan, Lesley Ames, and F. B. Tiffany, to draft a letter urging Eliot to stay in St. Paul. Citing Eliot's outstanding contributions to the church and community, the letter went on to say:

> For many years before you came, the church lived
> largely on its past, hopeful of the future, but maintained
> largely through the loyalty of a small and decreasing
> membership of the old guard. ... The man we had been
> hoping for came, and it is almost as if a new church has
> been born. We believe that your departure would be a
> disaster to Unity Church and to our movement in this
> part of the country.[61]

The minister was won over and remained with his parish.

In 1925 he was given a five-months' leave of absence to attend the hundredth anniversary of British and Foreign Unitarian churches in London. Mrs. Eliot accompanied him on this trip, and after the final meeting they traveled on the continent before returning home. (Ruth Kolling, parish assistant, assumed responsibility of the office.) For about two months of

---

[61] Minutes of the Board of Trustees May 9, 1923.

this period the supply minister was Dr. Albert Parker Fitch of Carleton College, who proved to be a tremendously popular speaker.

Twice more Eliot received tempting calls; the first came in 1926, from Cambridge, Massachusetts, where the First Parish Church earnestly desired Eliot to serve as Crothers' assistant minister. But once again, Unity Church members succeeded in persuading Eliot to remain with them. After Crothers' death in 1927, the Cambridge church made another attempt to secure Eliot's services, and when he rejected this offer, too, his congregation gave a rising vote of thanks to the minister and his wife. Also, as a token of appreciation the members raised $6,000, $2,000 of which was allocated for a sabbatical for the Eliots, the balance to be used to reduce the church mortgage. In retrospect it is interesting to read the "Message from the Minister," printed in the church bulletin of February 1928. In it, Eliot urged his parishioners (in return for his remaining with them), to strengthen their support of him in building up all phases of the church. This was essential, he felt, because:

> the restlessness and skepticism of our times do not provide an atmosphere congenial to the growth of institutional religion. There is grave doubt in many thoughtful minds as to whether the religion of the future will be expressed through any institutions at all.

Vital person that he was, Eliot found time aside from his ministerial duties to initiate vesper services and a series of radio talks. In addition, he authored three books during his St. Paul years: *The Fundamentals of Unitarian Faith*, *The Unwrought Iron* (for Sunday school use), and *Towards Belief in God*. He served on the boards of numerous social agencies, among them the Community Chest and the city welfare board. He had also been a member of the Board of Trustees of Mount Holyoke College and a director of the American Civil Liberties Union, to name just a few of his many varied activities. Awards came to him in the form of several honorary degrees, including those of Doctor of Laws from the University of Minnesota and Doctor of Divinity from Carleton College in Northfield, Minnesota.

The next step in Eliot's career has been outlined by Arthur Foote:

> During the depression years of the nineteen thirties, the Unitarian movement nationally was rent with theological controversy, and seemed badly bogged down with dwindling membership and lagging enthusiasm. Eliot, as minister of a thriving parish in marked contrast to this generally gloomy picture, was appointed chairman of an impressive Commission on Appraisal to study this situation and make recommendations for meeting it. Following the publication of the Commission's report, "Facing a New Age," Eliot became the obvious choice for the Presidency of the American Unitarian Association. Reluctant as he was to leave Unity Church, this "draft" was something he felt he could not decline, and he accepted election to this office in 1937.[62]

Wallace Robbins, who was to be the next minister of Unity Church, has said of his predecessor's work in this field that Eliot was largely instrumental in raising the American Unitarian Association from its low point of effectiveness, and also largely responsible for the explosion of the Unitarian membership.

Frederick Eliot actively carried on his work for the Association until his sudden death on February 16, 1958. A memorial service was held in Unity Church on October 1, 1961, at which time his former parishioners dedicated a bronze plaque to his memory. (The plaque now hangs on the South wall of the church foyer.) The addresses on that occasion were given by Harold E. Wood and Robbins. In recalling Eliot's most marked characteristics, Wood spoke of his compelling dignity; his great goodness and understanding; his disciplined mind; his quick temper; and his uproarious laugh. In conclusion Wood said, "He knew his people, young and old. No joy or sorrow was too slight for his immediate attention. ... For above all, he was a parish priest."

---

[62] Arthur Foote to Elinor S. Otto, June 4, 1971.

Figure 28 Frederick May Eliot
Minister of Unity Church 1917-1937
Minnesota Historical Society

VI. War Years and Recovery; Wallace W. Robbins and Arthur N. Foote 1937-1950

Frederick Eliot's departure ushered in a less comfortable period for Unity Church. The immediate question in 1937, was, of course, the selection of a new minister. The effects of the depression were still evidenced in reduced financial support, and most significantly, the threatening war and ultimate involvement of the United States created problems of a different nature: members of the congregation dispersed to other cities and into the war effort; gas rationing deterred members from attending church and transporting children to Sunday school; manpower was limited.

Until this time the standard procedure for selecting a minister had been by "serial candidating," a system whereby the candidates, chosen from a list compiled by the church, were invited to preach one at a time in the St. Paul pulpit. From this group, sometimes numbering as many as fifteen or twenty, a final choice was made. This method had many drawbacks. It was confusing to the voter, who did not necessarily hear every candidate (attendance in Unitarian churches being notably erratic), and, who, in any case, often could not in retrospect distinguish between them. As a general rule the last one heard was the best remembered. This frequently resulted in a haphazard selection, totally unfair to both candidate and parish. Also, the "popularity contest aspect" (as Arthur Foote has called it) of this method caused embarrassment to visiting ministers and occasionally created unpleasant factions within the church membership.

Consequently, the Unity Board devised a plan in which only one candidate at a time would be considered. This came to be known as the St. Paul Plan and was rapidly adopted by other Unitarian churches. It called for a fifteen-member General Committee divided into three sub-committees. To the Executive Committee, consisting of the chairman and two other members of the Board of Trustees, was delegated the authority to act for the Board, in the absence of a minister, on all matters pertaining to ministerial activities. The Committee on Permanent Supply was authorized to make a thorough search for the most suitable man.

This new approach allowed the candidate to be heard in his own church, or, by a prearranged invitation, in a nearby church, unaware that he was under scrutiny by an embassy from another congregation. Once selected as the candidate unanimously recommended to the congregation by the committee, the minister was invited to St. Paul for a week's visit, including two Sundays of preaching. The candidate's name was then presented to the congregation for a simple yes or no vote, and, in the event it was unfavorable, new committees were formed to explore further for another prospect. The third committee, on Temporary Supply, provided Sunday morning speakers for the period when the church was without a minister. (One of these guest speakers, at this time, was Lon Ray Call, who later served as interim minister during Arthur Foote's sabbatical leave in 1963-64.) This, with variations in number and size of committees, continues to be the accepted method of selection.

In their search for a mutually compatible minister, the committees carefully considered Eliot's admonition "to choose a minister with whom religion is the primary interest and to avoid a destructive radical."[63] The selected candidate, Wallace W. Robbins, of the Alton, Illinois, church, nicely fitted this description. He was highly recommended by Eliot, who had followed the younger man's career with interest.

Wallace Robbins was born in New Bedford, Massachusetts, in 1910. He spent his early years on a small farm which lay within the city limits and unhappily soon became a victim of urban development. His father managed a general store and actively participated in politics, serving as assessor, school committeeman, and tax collector. Robbins' grandfather, whose abhorrence of slavery had led him to volunteer in the Union

---

[63] Minutes of the Committee of Fifteen: February 19,1937. Unity Church (Saint Paul, Minn.). Unity Church records. Minnesota Historical Society.

Army, passed on to his grandson a firm tradition of devotion to human freedom, which became a guiding principle of Robbins' life.

After graduation from Tufts College in 1932 and Meadville Theological School in 1935, Robbins accepted a call from the First Unitarian Church of Alton, Illinois. In this first parish the young minister encountered two difficult situations. His predecessor's death by his own hand had left the congregation torn with self-accusations. In addition, the town's main industry was the manufacture of arms and munitions, which were at that time being shipped to Japan, and would, Robbins foresaw, eventually be turned against the Americans. There were some among his parishioners who sympathized with his humanitarian view that this traffic in weapons was morally reprehensible. But others were displeased by his denouncements of the industry and its policies and by his warnings of still greater evils to come out of the Nazi regime. Nevertheless, Robbins remained in Alton until 1938, when the invitation came to him from Unity Church.

The new minister was installed on June 1 of that same year, at which time, also, his predecessor's resignation became effective. Taking part in the service, in addition to Frederick Eliot, were Laurance R. Plank, First Unitarian Church of St. Louis, Robert E. Romig, First Unitarian Church of Duluth, and James L. Adams, professor of theology at the Meadville school. A rented parsonage at 945 Lincoln was made available for Robbins, his wife, Eleanor, and their then only child, Judith (Mrs. L. J. Faling). Subsequently a son, Jonathan, and another daughter, Sara (now Mrs. Robert MacLeod), were born.

Thirty-two years later, in June of 1970, Robbins, on one of his occasional return visits to Unity Church, remarked good humoredly that as he looked back on his earlier days in that same pulpit, he could appreciate the wisdom shown in choosing a youthful minister to succeed Eliot, because a young man's mistakes are more readily forgiven. Certainly, in accepting the call to Unity Church, Robbins, like other past ministers, was confronted with a difficult task: that of maintaining his own

Figure 29 Wallace W. Robbins, 1938-1944
Photograph by the St. Paul Dispatch-Pioneer Press

integrity and pursuing his own goals in the face of the inevitable comparisons between a new and a well-established preceding ministry.

Nevertheless, the young minister soon demonstrated a fine facility for understanding contemporary needs while retaining many traditions of the past. A resonant voice, commanding appearance in the pulpit, delightful sense of humor, and talent as a raconteur are some of the traits his parishioners came to know.

Like his predecessor, Robbins himself undertook direction of the Sunday school. Assisting him were the director of instruction and the chairman of the Church School Committee. This structure prevailed until 1944, when Mrs. A. H. Sargent became superintendent of the church school, filling the interim between Robbins' resignation and the installation of Arthur Foote.

One of Robbins' greatest interests revolved around young adults, and his relationship with them was particularly successful. Tower Club grew stronger and more popular, stimulated by the planning of its own programs and the variety of subjects brought up for discussion. The little room in the tower was now outgrown and abandoned. In 1943 the senior Sunday school class was eliminated entirely, and its members were absorbed into the older group.

Two other social organizations for young people took shape. The Channing Club, established for married couples, concentrated on work projects within the church. The Forum, open to men and women of college age, was an informal discussion group meeting with the minister in his study. Equally successful with these and older age levels were the excellent classes by Robbins on the Bible and Bible history.

Wallace Robbins had found that few of the younger women members were available to assist in church activities because they were all so busily engaged in volunteer work outside the parish. To entice the women back into church participation, Robbins and Mrs. John Locke proposed the formation of the Minister's Guild, specifically designed to lend the minister a helping hand. Often throughout the years the Guild has been asked to carry out special requests of the minister, but its greatest contribution has been the maintenance of a contingency fund, for use by the minister at his discretion. Money for this project has been earned from bazaars, fairs, and a variety of other profit-making schemes. Established in 1941, under the presidency of Mrs. Henry H. Cowie, the Guild has now been in existence for thirty years.

Until the depression and the stringencies of the war began to pinch the church financially, the office staff had consisted of a secretary, Elizabeth Buckley; a director of activities, Mrs. John Locke; and two lay assistants. (Her title, Mrs. Locke says, covered a multitude of duties, including one on-the-spot hemming of a robe borrowed from Robbins for use by a considerably smaller visiting minister.) When Miss Buckley left for Boston to assist Eliot in 1939, the office duties were assumed by Miss Mary Turner (Mrs. John Kenna), a granddaughter of Charles W. Ames. She held this position for over ten years.

However, in 1940 the financial state of the church reached its lowest point in some time. Several years earlier Eliot had accepted a cut in salary, and now the Board of Trustees was forced to further curtail the budget and salaries. Robbins received a salary of $4,400 out of a total budget of $13,798. Mrs. Locke's job was turned over to volunteer members of the congregation. As an additional economy the choir also became a volunteer group, and Mrs. Snyder, whose fine directing and singing had enhanced the Sunday services, was not rehired when her contract expired in 1941. Fortunately, three years later the organist, Mrs. Louis H. Powell, the former Virginia Wetherbee, assumed the leadership of the choir and the high quality of church music was maintained.

Postwar restrictions influenced other phases of church life. Since only the most essential building activity was permitted, Unity Church was obliged to postpone any plans for expansion. The bequest of Miss Hester Pollock (1942), designated specifically for redecorating the church sanctuary and rebuilding the organ, was placed in a reserve fund and not utilized until 1949-51.

Figure 30 Virginia Wetherbee Powell
Choir Director and Organist, 1928-1980

Use of the kitchen and adjacent rooms by the St. Paul Academy Junior School for the luncheon hour was permitted, to ease its own cramped situation. But this arrangement proved unsatisfactory and was terminated after a few years. On the other hand, renting of space to the women of the New Century Club for afternoon programs was so successful that, thirty years later, the club members are still bimonthly occupants of the parish hall.

Perceptive to the changing mores, Robbins recognized that Sundays had become as important for family recreation as for churchgoing. To enable families to enjoy this day together as well as to benefit those who for valid reasons had missed church, Robbins experimented with an additional service held at eight o'clock on Wednesday evenings. In so far as possible these duplicated the Sunday morning services. It was an appreciated venture Robbins also maintained the practice of twice-yearly communion services, a pattern set by Eliot. (This custom was continued into Arthur Foote's ministry until 1964.

Five communion services were held during the year, always at times other than the regular Sunday morning service.)

Naturally the parish was deeply concerned for its young people actively involved in World War II. Robbins and a committee of women, under the chairmanship of Mrs. Charles Sommers, alternated in writing newsletters to every member on military duty. A red lamp, symbol of courage and human brotherhood, was placed in the church chancel. It burned continuously throughout the war years "to remind all people of the men and women of the church serving in the armed forces and of the four who gave their lives in the conflict."

But neither war nor hard times could entirely suppress the party-giving spirit at Unity Church. One particularly lively event was a Russian War Relief party in December of 1943, the purpose of which was to collect clothing for our then allies. Each guest, having donned as many layers of garments as possible, proceeded, in a reasonable facsimile of a strip-tease act, to peel off one excess layer after another. The prize was given (as proclaimed in the program), "for the maximum discarded, not the minimum which remains." The action was accompanied by the burlesque chant, "Take it off," and the participants were encouraged by the doggerel written by James Gray (St. Paul columnist). Robbins' contemporaries may remember the nonsense of the verses:

> There's a quiet little church where the lib'rals love to go
> To be shorn of their hatreds and prejudices low.
> The minister fears ornaments of bigoted display
> And boy! how he strips 'em all away.
>
> "Take it off—take it off," cries the pastor, firm and kind,
> "Take it off—take it off," it clutters up your mind.
> And we always obey him,
> Even though we may be slow
> And emerge, with innocence aglow.
>
> The refrain, gently poking fun at the flourishing red
> beard Robbins had grown during the summer (twenty

years in the forefront of the fashion), leads into the final
verse.

"Take it off—take it off," cried Miss Furness from the
rear.
"Leave it on—leave it on," said Miss Laura. "It's a dear."
But he's always obliging,
If the truth is not at stake,
So he shaved for sweet tradition's sake.

Now they're giving a mad party to help the Russians
live. They'd give their shirts for freedom, so their shirts
are what they give,
Not to mention the underwear against the winds that
nip So sing a song of battle while they strip.

"Take it off—take it off," cries Stalin from the steppes.
"Take it off—take it off," echoes Mr. Turner, Epes.
So we give of our faith
And also of our pants
To freedom, as soon as fortune grants.

In spite of such occasional frivolity, the stress and tragedy of
these times were later acknowledged by Robbins when he
visited St. Paul in 1970. Although not an absolute pacifist
Robbins did hold that in the years before the actual outbreak of
the war the United States had demonstrated neglect in not
standing firmly against Nazi Germany and Fascist Italy on all
possible grounds of the moral issues involved. This attitude was
met with some misunderstanding. His sympathy for victims of
the war led him to organize the first and only attempt by
Christians in St. Paul to care for German-Jewish refugees, who
needed assistance in beginning a new life.

At the same time, through his friendship with Clarence
Mitchell, then executive secretary of the Urban League,
Robbins became acutely aware of the needs of the city's
minority groups. As early as 1939 he was elected to the
presidency of the Urban League, and for many years he and
Harry Huse were the only white men willing to serve on the

board of this organization. It was largely through Robbins' influence that Unity Church for the first time in its history became actively involved in the welfare and racial problems of the black people. He received some support from a few members of the church, among them Mrs. Harry Palmer who was vitally interested in the Hallie Q. Brown Center. The Minister's Guild also contributed in various ways. But much of this was an uphill struggle because many citizens had not as yet become aroused to racial inequities and some church members as well as civic leaders were unsympathetic to any efforts towards remedial action.

In other areas also Robbins made substantial contributions. He was chairman of the Municipal Housing Commission and was appointed to the mayor's Committee on Slum Clearance in St. Paul. Serving on this same committee was George Morgan, a lawyer and a member of Unity Church, whose knowledge and wisdom Robbins acknowledges to have been of great benefit to him personally and to the work of this organization. The minister's familiarity with the city's social affairs led to many requests for his services as an arbitrator in management-labor disputes, which in turn resulted in his appointment by Harold Stassen to the Minnesota Governor's Wartime Labor Panel. Subsequently, Robbins was selected to serve on the United States War Labor Panel, where his diplomacy enabled him to play a decisive role in arbitration. He was also active in the Foreign Policy Association and just before leaving St. Paul he had begun laying the foundation for a Committee on Human Relations, a program in which Warren Burger (then of St. Paul and now Chief Justice of the Supreme Court) took considerable interest.

But once again it was Unity Church's fate to lose its minister to an important post in a broader field. Just short of six years after his installation Robbins was elected president of the Meadville Theological Seminary, and with deep regret his parishioners accepted his resignation. On February 16, 1944, Charles Sommers said in expressing the congregation's appreciation for Robbins' achievements outside the church as well as within it:

Never has the church had as its minister, one who in such a short space of time, has won for himself higher respect from the denomination, or carried a larger share of responsibilities for the welfare of the entire community.

Wallace Robbins remained president of the Meadville school for twelve years. He has been the recipient of various honors, including the degree of Doctor of Sacred Theology from Tufts College (1947) and the Butler Professorship from the University of Chicago. He was associate dean at the Rockefeller Memorial Chapel, University of Chicago, and has been on the Board of Preachers of both Harvard and Wellesley colleges. In 1956 he accepted a call to the First Unitarian Church in Worcester, Massachusetts, a parish he is currently serving.

Committees to select another minister immediately went into action, with minor changes introduced into the one-candidate plan. In order to represent all possible viewpoints, the General Committee was enlarged to twenty members, including one each from the Minister's Guild, the Elizabeth Eliot Club, the Women's Alliance, and the Tower Club. The Permanent Supply Committee was increased from three to five, and a subcommittee appointed to arrange for appropriate entertainment of the visiting minister. The chairmen of the committees were Louis S. Headley, Permanent Supply; Charles L. Sommers, Temporary Supply; and Chandler B. Davis, Executive Committee.

The successor to Wallace Robbins was a man whose name was already known to these committees, and who, in Robbins' opinion, was ideally suited to fill the St. Paul pulpit. In fact, when asked by Mrs. William West, Jr., if he could recommend a candidate for Unity Church, Robbins smilingly replied that he knew just the man. He had been a fellow student at Meadville Theological School, he was presently at Stockton, California, and his name was Arthur N. Foote II.

In making the actual selection, however, the church deviated from the new plan. No reason for this is given, but the plausible explanation seems to lie in the committee's eagerness to secure Foote as the next minister. Without waiting to go through the usual candidating procedures, the Permanent Supply Committee arranged with the Temporary Supply Committee to invite Arthur Foote to preach at Unity Church in the fall of 1944. Foote twice declined, correctly assuming that although the invitation said nothing about candidating, this was what the committee had in mind. He admits that he was reluctant even to consider the St. Paul offer, having set his sights on the upcoming vacancies in the parishes at San Francisco and Berkeley. But he finally consented to come to Unity Church in December, and of this experience he says frankly, "It was an enviable way to candidate, placing the congregation in the position of having to prove to me that I ought to accept."[64]

The committees and the congregation obviously did convince Foote of the desirability of the job because when the vote ran overwhelmingly in his favor, he accepted the call to St. Paul. Since he had already preached at Unity Church on two successive Sundays, it seemed unnecessary to recall him from California for a special appearance.

A first message from the new minister to his congregation, appearing in the bulletin of March 9, 1945, gave some indication of the kind of independent man the parish had chosen:

> You know, of course, that I am not my predecessor. We happen to be old friends and share many convictions and beliefs. But I am I... and I shall not attempt to be Wallace Robbins....So I hope you will accept me for what I am, and will not try to compare us. You will want me to maintain my own integrity and be as true as I can to my own ideals."

---

[64] Arthur Foote to Elinor S. Otto, April 3, 1971.

Figure 31 Arthur N. Foote II
Minister of Unity from 1945-1970
About 1960, Photograph by the St. Paul Dispatch-Pioneer Press

A letter written in a less serious mood on May 4 says:

> I am thirty-four years old, not yet bald or pot-bellied,
> and of cheerful disposition. My principal asset is my
> wife, Rebecca.... We have been living in Stockton,
> California, where I was the minister not only of the
> Stockton church, but also that of the one in
> Sacramento—a kind of Unitarian circuit rider for the
> whole San Joaquin Valley.

The eleventh minister of Unity Church, Arthur Foote is the third to have come from a Unitarian background. In fact, his family has been prominently associated with the Unitarian movement for three generations. His father and grandfather, both named Henry Wilder Foote, were Unitarian ministers, his father also having been a professor in the Harvard Divinity School. Foote's paternal grandmother was the sister of Harvard's famous president, Charles W. Eliot. He is also the great-nephew and namesake of the distinguished organist and composer, Arthur Foote. His Quaker mother was Eleanor Tyson Cope of Germantown, Pennsylvania.

Arthur Foote was born in Ann Arbor, Michigan, in 1911. He completed his undergraduate work at Harvard College in 1933, where he showed prowess as a long-distance runner, one summer competing with the combined Harvard-Yale team against a Cambridge-Oxford team in England. Foote also traveled widely, visiting Unitarian churches in England, Ireland, Czechoslovakia, and Transylvania. After earning his B.D. from Meadville Theological School in 1936, Foote was ordained in his grandfather's church, King's Chapel, Boston, and then, preferring to work in an unfamiliar region, he accepted the dual ministry of the two small California churches.

During his stay there, from 1936-45, he participated in organizations whose goals and purposes have concerned him throughout his life. He was a member of the board of Starr King School for the Ministry; regional vice-president of the Unitarian Fellowship for Social Justice and the Unitarian Pacifist Fellowship; and Stockton representative of the American Civil Liberties Union. In addition, his musical ability brought him membership in the American Guild of Organists. His wife, the former Rebecca Clark of Southwest Harbor, Maine, attended the University of Maine, and, after her marriage, Lewis Institute in Chicago. They have three children, Frances Eliot (now Mrs. C. J. Stehman, Jr.), Nathan Clark, and Caleb.

Soon after the minister and his family arrived in St. Paul, they were proudly presented with the first Unity Church-owned parsonage. The house at 764 Goodrich was purchased for $10,000, over half of which was raised by subscriptions, the remainder from the church's reserve fund and by means of a mortgage.

Arthur Foote preached the first sermon from his new pulpit on April 15, 1945. On October 21 he was installed. The service was especially memorable because the installation prayer and the sermon were delivered by his father. The invocation prayer was given by Raymond B. Bragg of the First Unitarian Society of Minneapolis, the charge to the minister by Frederick Eliot, and the charge to the congregation by Wallace Robbins.

Within the first five years of the new ministry two organizations came into existence:

1. The Crothers Club (1946), which has been active from time to time throughout the succeeding years, was a social and discussion group for young adults.
2. The 50-100 Club, established in 1949, was open to married couples whose combined ages totaled between 50 and 100. The prime movers in starting this group were the John Bergstedts, who had belonged to a similar club in their former Kansas City church and considered it a valuable type of church organization. Its purpose was primarily to help the members become better acquainted, but it also assumed work projects for the church. In the 1950's the members participated in some community services, providing chaperones for teen-age dances at the Park Christian Center (a recreational facility for young people in the Dale-Selby area), and sponsoring two war refugees, Mila and Lazlo Ambrus, both of whom were medical doctors. (Lazlo Ambrus was a Transylvanian Unitarian.)

As concerned the church structure, the problems seemed to be perennial ones. The often-maligned stained-glass windows were badly in need of repair (or preferably, replacement); the kitchen was inadequate; the Sunday school was bursting at the seams. The more than $13,000 in the Hester Pollock fund remained unused because of the housing emergency codes still in effect. But, finally, in 1949, some of this money was committed to the redecorating of the sanctuary. Under the direction of Miss Helen Bunn's committee, the walls were painted, a new lectern and pulpit which had been commissioned earlier from Yungbauer and Sons were installed, and the pew cushions were recovered. None of this, however, answered the need for additional space for the rapidly growing church population and for more assistance for the minister in his increasingly demanding parish work.

Figure 32 Elizabeth M. Whitman
Director of Religious Education, 1948-1972
Photograph by Henry Hall

No remedy for the cramped quarters was to be feasible for several years to come, but as luck would have it, two women visiting over a fence solved the question of the minister's helper. Rebecca Foote, chatting with her neighbor, Mrs. Albert Whitman, unearthed the information that the Whitman daughter was a trained religious education director. Miss Elizabeth Whitman, a Vassar graduate, with an M.A. in religious education from Union Theological Seminary, was at the time directing the large church school of the Congregational First Christ Church in Longmeadow, Massachusetts. To the great good fortune of the Unitarians, she accepted the offer of an equivalent position in St. Paul, and on November 14, 1948, she was installed. Three lay members of the church were asked to assist in the service; Harry G. Huse, Mrs. James Holman, and John J. Schlenck, Sr. To date, in the more than twenty years of Miss Whitman's exceptional directorship, the Sunday school has not only quadrupled in numbers, but has undergone many adjustments in concepts, methods, and programs adapted to the size of the school and the changing philosophies of religious teaching.

Under the equally excellent leadership of Mrs. Powell, music for the Sunday services maintained its high standards, and now a majority of the fifteen choir positions were filled by members of Unity Church. It was the church's rare good fortune, moreover, to have a minister who was also a musician and a composer, a fact which promoted interest in the church music and in the growth of the music library. The descants, anthems, introits, and responses composed by Foote were frequent, much-admired adjuncts to the service. The Music Committee obviously felt that some very worthwhile musical moments were being squandered on a meager group of early Sunday morning arrivals. Its report of January 29, 1947 urged the churchgoers, "now that Mr. Foote has succeeded in getting the congregation here on time," to come a little earlier still to avail themselves of the introductory musical offerings. As usual, according to the same report, the quality of the parishioners' hymn singing left much to be desired.
Since that time many musical events have taken place at Unity Church. A number of concerts were given throughout the fifties

and sixties, among them performances by the church choir, the Schubert Club, the Flor Quartet, the St. Paul pianist, Mrs. Marjorie Winslow Briggs, and rousing presentations of "S. S. Pinafore" and "Iolanthe" by choir members. In recent years the sanctuary has, on occasion, echoed with the music of "rock" groups. This undoubtedly would have astounded even Kristofer Janson, who, in 1890, had so angrily defended the performing of Chopin's waltzes within the church walls.

The annual reports of the late forties reveal several incidents, not in themselves momentous, but interesting because of their contemporary social or political nature and because of the church's stand on them. In 1948 the Unitarian Service Committee (and consequently the leadership of AUA), was accused by a group called the Committee of Free Unitarians of being communistic. Foote asked for and received from the Board and members of the church a resolution supporting the Unitarian Service Committee and Eliot's administration in the face of this attack. In the same year Unity Church adopted a resolution urging President Truman to formulate and pass measures implementing the recommendations of his report "To Secure These Rights," and in so doing, the members pledged their co-operation in the abolition of prejudice and their support of the Civil Rights program.

The following year, the League for Democratic Socialism was permitted to rent the church basement for a meeting. Several newspaper articles were published in which Unity Church was made to appear as the sponsor for this group, and as a result of adverse publicity on this issue, the Board of Trustees deemed it necessary to establish specific guidelines relative to any further rental of church space.

Unquestionably the most important contemporary achievement in the field of social action was the transformation of Minnesota's mental hospitals. The credit for this accomplishment belongs largely to a handful of Unitarians whose initiative and perseverance helped to raise the state from the rank of thirty seventh to nearly, if not actually, the top in the nation as regards standards of psychiatric care for mental patients. Moreover, nationwide recognition came to the Unitarians because of the efforts of these few individuals.

The first move in this direction was made in 1946 by Miss Engla Schey, an attendant at Hastings Hospital, who, by presenting a conference of the Minnesota Unitarian Association with the facts about the abusive handling of patients, persuaded this group to pass a resolution authorizing an investigation of state institutions. Mrs. Lawrence Steefel (a former social worker and a member of Unity Church) took the next step by enlisting such experts as the head of the University of Minnesota Medical School and the director of the state's institutions to work with an investigating committee, chaired by Arthur Foote.

A further and decisive push was given to the program when Foote, in an off-the-cuff statement to a small meeting, asserted that the findings of the committee included the discovery that doctors were signing commitment papers for patients they had never seen. The unexpected presence of a newspaper reporter brought this comment to the attention of the public and also brought an angry response from Governor Luther Youngdahl. But data collected by the committee and confirmed by the governor's first visit to the Fergus Falls hospital—a visit instigated by Foote—convinced Youngdahl of the appalling conditions and treatment of the patients. Not only were the hospitals found to be outrageously understaffed (one doctor to seven hundred patients), but among other abuses, the use of shackles and straitjackets was prevalent, the diet of the patients was substandard while the staff ate well, and no psychiatric treatment was available for cure or rehabilitation. An initial result of the interview with the governor was his invitation to Foote to serve on his recently named Governor's Advisory Council on Mental Health (1947), which consisted of seven psychiatrists and one layman, Frank Rarig, Jr. (director of the Wilder Charities of St. Paul and a member of Unity Church). This council proceeded to draw up a series of recommendations for radically upgrading the state's mental institutions.

With this impetus to the program Minnesota became the first state to adopt a new approach towards the care of mental patients in placing the emphasis on the cure or rehabilitation of the patient rather than simply on confinement. Youngdahl's forceful campaign for a by now well-publicized cause brought about the establishment of a Citizens' Mental Health Committee (1948) and proposals for legislative action to improve hospital conditions. Bills passed in the Legislature of 1949 included an appropriation of $30,000,000 for care and treatment of patients as well as for a building program. The governor's recommendations covered increases in staff, research programs, training of personnel, and the mandatory requirement of a single diet for patients and staff. (Minnesota thereby became the first state to initiate this practice, too.) Robert Esbjornson in his book, *A Christian in Politics: Luther Youngdahl*, gives full credit to the Unitarian group for its role in the movement. In fact, the author states, "Apart from the work of the Unitarian Committee on Mental Health, there is no evidence that the Protestant churches made a concerted effort, either collectively or singly, to bring about this legislation."[65]

But this dedicated handful of Unitarians, not content with the measures undertaken up to this point, assumed the job of "gadfly" to oversee the total program and to insure the continuation of the progress already achieved. In order to ascertain the extent of improvement under Youngdahl's program, Arthur Foote and Josephine Downey, a member of the Elizabeth Eliot Club, spent a week, working incognito, as attendants at Anoka Hospital. One group, composed of doctors and lawyers from Unity Church, reviewed the processes by which the mentally ill were "tried" in the courts, in an effort to bring about change in this inhuman method of commitment.

Other St. Paul Unitarians, in addition to their minister and Mrs. Steefel, the indefatigable secretary of the committee, whose involvement in this program helped to contribute to its success, were Miss Elsa Krauch, Miss Phyllis Mickelson, Louis

---

[65] Robert Esbjornson, *A Christian in Politics: Luther W. Youngdahl* (Minneapolis: T.S. Denison, 1955), 181.

Schuldt, Mrs. Perrin Stryker, Mrs. Oscar Sullivan, Mrs. David Thorsen, and Don Wilson.

Subsequently, a number of new committees were established as outgrowths of these initial moves and Foote, who had already earned the title of "the father of mental health in Minnesota," continued to play an important part in the program. In addition to serving as chairman of the Minnesota Unitarian Conference Mental Hospital Committee and as vice-president of the Minnesota Mental Health Association (1953-56), he was named (by Governor Youngdahl) chairman of a committee of doctors and lawyers on commitment law revision (1951-53). Foote also served on the Governor's Advisory Council on Mental Health until it was disbanded shortly after Youngdahl was appointed to the federal bench in 1954. In 1961 Governor Elmer L. Andersen named him to serve again on this advisory council.

Meanwhile several members of the Elizabeth Eliot Club had begun making regular visits to the state hospital for the men tally ill at Hastings. Among the chief promoters of this undertaking was Elsa Krauch, author of *A Mind Restored*, one of the first books written about life in a mental hospital. Thereafter, for nearly twenty years these women faithfully made monthly trips to Hastings, loading their cars with some of the hundreds of magazines that had been collected at the church, and putting on song fests, bingo and birthday parties. They comprised the first group in the state—almost in the nation—to carry out this kind of work for the benefit of mental patients. (A group from the Minneapolis Unitarian Society also undertook a similar project at Anoka State Hospital.)

In 1956, the Elizabeth Eliot Club initiated a second program which was a piece of significant social pioneering in the field of after-care for those in mental hospitals, and one which has since been widely followed in Minnesota and elsewhere. Backed financially by the Elizabeth Eliot Club, four of its members, Mrs. Ethel Jenkins, Miss Olga Skinvik, Miss Josephine Downey, and Mrs. Elsie Worch aided a group of former mental patients to establish their own Amity Club. For a time, and through a grant from the Hill Family Foundation, the services of a trained worker were enlisted. Mrs. Ida Davies, a Minneapolis Unitarian, assisted by the Elizabeth Eliot Club members, created an active and helpful group which met regularly at Unity Church.

The concern and constancy of these women on behalf of the mentally ill has earned deserved praise from Arthur Foote who wrote, "of all the church organizations, I would have to put the Elizabeth Eliot Club first in terms of its members' patient and consistent labors for others."[66]

Towards the end of the decade, in 1947, Unity Church reached an important milestone, its 75th anniversary. For this gala occasion, celebrated on February 25, both Frederick Eliot and Wallace Robbins were on hand. Richard Boynton, the only other former minister still living, was unable to attend.

The evening's entertainment was under the direction of Mrs. Cushing Wright (Margaret Ames). It opened with the appearance of Louis Headley, who, dressed as Frederick R. Newell, narrated a light-hearted history of Unity Church as seen through the eyes of the earlier Unitarian figure. The story was occasionally interspersed with historical comment by Mary Chapin (Mrs. George Heisig), portraying Emma Kelley. Headley's narrative was followed by a series of "Living Pictures," a succession of tableaux in which church members, costumed in the dress of previous times, posed singly within a large gold frame to resemble portraits of their forebears. The models and their originals included: Mrs. James Holman as her grandmother, Mrs. Charles Clark; Mrs. Henry Randall as her mother, Mrs. George Sommers; Charles Lesley Ames as his father, Charles Wilberforce Ames; Chandler Davis as Anderson Wimbish; Walter Chapin, Jr., as his grandfather, George Chapin. As a finale to the program the curtain rose on Arthur and Rebecca Foote posed together in a portrait of themselves.

---

[66] Arthur Foote to Elinor S. Otto, August 7, 1971.

But as the church celebrated its seventy-five years of steady progress from a very precarious beginning in 1872, it was facing a new kind of challenge, that of how to cope with a congregation rapidly outgrowing its present accommodations and already too large to be ministered to by one man. It was in the succeeding decade that this challenge was met.

VII. Growth and Expansion 1950-1960

The 1950's were a time of general church growth throughout the country, due in part to the wartime "baby boom." And in the first year of this decade the necessity for more "lebensraum" at Unity Church had already become acute. Elizabeth Whitman reported that all available space, including the dining-room and assembly room, were in use by the children's classes. In 1951 church school enrollment stood at 175, and four years later the number topped 300. A similar increase in church membership is shown by the statistics. The average attendance in 1950 was 196; it rose to 280 in 1954 and by 1956 the voting membership had reached 615.

To ease the situation a number of measures were introduced. For a while the church rented the classrooms in the St. Paul Academy Junior School across the street on Portland Avenue. The church school program was augmented to two sessions of classes and four chapel services. Even the Christmas pageant was affected by the population growth, which necessitated limiting membership in the cast to specified age groups. The overflow audience standing in the aisles on Christmas Eve constituted a fire hazard, and the church was compelled to add a dress rehearsal performance given on the previous evening. The sanctuary was still able to accommodate the Sunday morning congregation, except on Easter when a second service became necessary to house the traditional spring outburst.

Since it was the bulging Sunday school that was in the most urgent need of room the church members voted to remodel the basement in accordance with the plans of the architect, Magnus Jemne. By radically altering the then existing dining hall and partitioning the resulting space, six additional classrooms were made available. The $8,400 project was partially financed by funds from the $10,000 bequest of Miss Helen Bunn.

But this was merely a stopgap measure and by 1953 it was generally conceded that Unity Church had arrived at a crucial point in its growth. In order to determine what course the church should now follow, a fifteen-member Planning Commission, headed by Orville C. Peterson, was appointed to thoroughly explore the future of Unity Church and Unitarianism in St. Paul. A long-range plan was then submitted to the parish on October 13, 1954, and subsequently neighborhood meetings were held to allow every parishioner to hear and discuss the proposals of the commission. The following points were considered:

1. While membership growth was a healthy indication, it was possible that the church might soon pass its optimum size. (In fact, it was the opinion of Foote and some members that this point had already been passed.)
2. Was the solution the formation of a second Unitarian church in St. Paul?
3. Should a larger church be erected at a new site?
4. Should the church remain at the present location and construct additional office and classroom space?
5. Should the church add a second minister to the staff?

As was to be expected, some members, trusting that the numerical peak in church growth had already been reached, favored the "status quo," but the commission maintained that a "do nothing" attitude was neither consistent with a dynamic church nor conducive to spiritual growth. The arguments against building a larger church at a new site were conclusive. Of most significance was the strong feeling on the part of the minister and many of the members that a church should not abandon a deteriorating neighborhood for a more prosperous area (as other churches had done) but should share the responsibility of contributing to the betterment of its community. Practical factors, too, were taken into consideration. The present structure was reasonably adequate, physically and aesthetically, the present location was convenient for the majority of the parish (two-thirds of whom lived within the triangle bounded by Seventh Street, Marshall Avenue, and the Mississippi River); the cost of construction was unreasonably high, and the resale of church property notoriously poor. Also, not to be overlooked were the disadvantages of an even larger congregation, in particular the inevitable weakening of the minister's relationship with his parishioners.

The establishment of a "branch," on the other hand, had much in its favor. Although the formation of a second church within the Unitarian-concentrated area already mentioned could lead to serious competition, this second church in another location might help to stem the growth of Unity Church. Moreover, since the Unitarian "saturation point" had not yet been reached in St. Paul, and since there was only one Unitarian church in the city, a "branch" in an outlying, rapidly developing area (such as the north or east rim of the city), would make Unitarianism available to those not served by the existing church. As one member of the commission expressed it, "[We are] interested in colonization, not deportation."[67]

As a result of its findings the Planning Commission recommended three steps which would ease Unity Church's attack of growing pains:
1. The present building should be retained, and an addition constructed to provide the needed offices and class rooms;
2. the establishment of a second church in an outlying area should be encouraged;
3. another minister should be added to the staff to assist Foote in the increasing responsibilities of a large membership.

The first step in these directions was taken by Chandler B. Davis and John D. Barwise (of the Land Acquisition Committee) who were authorized to investigate the purchasing of the property on Portland Avenue to the east of the church or the property to the north on the corner of Grotto Street and Holly Avenue. The latter site was recommended by Jemne (consulting architect for the Architectural Planning Committee), because this property afforded a larger building area and because an addition at the rear of the existing church would not necessarily have to match the older portion, thereby

---

[67] Report of the Planning Commission, October 13, 1954.

112

involving less expense. Construction at this location, however, did entail turning the alley, for which permission from the city and from homeowners in the block was needed. The alley, running east and west, divided the south lot on Portland (site of the existing church) from the north lot on Holly (site of the proposed wing). In order to join the two structures, the alley had to be closed at the east boundary of the church property and a new exit made onto Holly. The actual purchase of these properties was accomplished in October 1955, at a cost of $40,000.

The next move was up to the Finance Advisory Board, whose members included William West, Jr., chairman; Harry Huse, Harold Wood, Chandler Davis, and Harry G. Barnes. And here the Unitarians ran into some of what Wallace Robbins once called "their honest differences." Because the sum of money to be raised was large, the Board of Trustees recommended hiring a professional fund-raising organization. Several such companies were interviewed. But a number of independent-minded members were convinced that the parish could achieve the goal without outside assistance. So, with sturdy Unitarian conviction, this group petitioned for a special meeting to debate the issue. In preference to holding an extra session, however, the Board turned over the annual meeting on January 8, 1956, to the proponents of the "Campaign on a Do-It-Ourselves Basis." Both sides were ably defended, and the meeting proved to be a slightly heated one. The matter was settled by a vote of 87-66 in favor of a nonprofessionally-managed fund drive, but a proviso was added that, if by February 1, further investigation indicated that this was not feasible, the Board of Trustees was authorized to hire a professional group. B. Warner Shippee, spokesman for the "Do-It-Ourselves" cause, became chairman of the building fund campaign, with his supporter, Harold Wood, as co-chairman.

Differences of opinion were quickly dissipated in an unusually lively drive to raise the necessary money. The opening event was set for April 20, 1956, and both Frederick Eliot and Wallace Robbins spoke. Unfortunately, the details of the program for this occasion are not recorded. But contemporaries have memories of the standing-room-only audience in the Macalester College gymnasium and of Harold Wood's usual skillful performance as master of ceremonies. The witty script, centering around a projection fifty years into the future, contained abundant timely gibes at Unitarians in general, individual members of Unity Church in particular, and other aspects of church affairs, including fund raising, committees on committees, and the Christmas pageant controversy (described later).

One portion of the program predominates in the reminiscences of contemporary spectators, one of whom gave this account:

> A sudden commotion in the back of the hall announced the entrance of an elderly man in a wheel chair, propelled by a supposed intern in a white coat. Attached to the chair were all the appurtenances for a transfusion—a frame holding a jar, with a variety of tubes leading from it. The old gentleman and the attendant sped down the length of the aisle to the speakers' table, and the patient (characterized by spry, eighty-six-year-old Charles Sommers), managed to gasp, "I want to subscribe to the fund before I pass on."

Meanwhile, the Committee on Architectural Planning also had Bratnober, chairman; Miss Perrie Jones, Hamilton Ross, and Magnus Jemne (ex-officio). Somewhat later five women were added to the committee; Mrs. Emil Nelson, Mrs. Edward Brooks, Mrs. W. H. Alderman, Mrs. George Reisig, and Mrs. Albert Arny; the latter three serving as a subcommittee to consult in planning the kitchen. The architect chosen was Richard Hammel, a partner in the St. Paul firm of Hammel and Green. Specifications for the new wing were incorporated in the minutes of the Board of Trustees' meeting, February 15, 1956, as quoted here:

> Alterations—A new stairway will be in the location of Mr. Foote's present office. The office suite will become a choir room and an office for the choir director. Remodeling in the basement will remove the kitchen and provide three additional classrooms....

114

New Building—The new building is to be two stories high with a total area of 10,500 square feet on the two floors, exterior facing material of brick, aluminum windows, and a flat built-up roof. It will be 66' x 66' joined to the present building by a link 22' x 44'. The kitchen will be in this link and will serve into the present parish hall and new multi-purpose room.... With the new building the church will have a total of 26 classrooms.

The addition was to be so constructed that another floor could be added later, if desired. Total cost of the project including architectural fees and equipment came to approximately $240,000. A loan of $110,000 at 5%, to be retired by 1960, was arranged with the First National Bank of St. Paul.

Actual construction began in November of 1956, and by the following October, the building was in use. The final touch was added five years later when a plaque placed on the wall outside the center room of the wing designated that the new addition had appropriately been named in memory of Frederick May Eliot. In fact, no other name for the wing had even been considered. Unfortunately, the news was not relayed to Eliot in time for him to know of this decision. The plaque carries the names of many members and friends in whose memory gifts had been made. The Center Room was made possible by a contribution in memory of the C. C. DeCosters, and the fireplace was given in memory of Helen Bunn.

But Arthur Foote, lest his parishioners take inordinate pride only in the material matters of the church, took the opportunity in his annual report on October 28, 1957, to offer a gentle admonition, when he said, "We have a wonderful new tool with which to be about our business, which is not building walls, but people."

Nevertheless, one other acquisition of several years earlier deserves mention. By 1951 parking problems near the church had become acute. The church was informed by Theodore W. Koch that the tax-forfeited property on the northwest corner of Portland Avenue and St. Albans Street was for sale and about to be purchased as the site of an apartment building, thereby removing the last open space in the nearby area. By acting promptly, a Parking Lot Committee, headed by Koch, succeeded in buying the property and persuading the neighboring home owners to permit the use of it for parking. The church at this juncture had no funds available for improving the lot, but a special fund-raising committee obtained the entire necessary amount of $4,300. At Koch's death, in 1962, renovation of the parking lot was made possible through the gifts contributed in his memory to the Unity Church Memorial Fund.

The Board of Trustees had not been ignoring the other recommendations of the Planning Commission, that is, to call an associate minister and to encourage those Unitarians who evinced interest in a "branch" church. As to the first of these proposals, the Board and Arthur Foote concluded that it was more practical to add an assistant rather than an associate minister to the staff. The choice fell on Ronald J. Walrath, a recent graduate of Syracuse University and Meadville Theological School. Walrath had also been a student assistant at the People's Church in Chicago. He was hired on a one-year probationary period, at a salary of $4,000 plus housing and gas allowances. His contract (on the same basis as Foote's and Miss Whitman's) called for an indeterminate tenure with ninety days' notice. Since he was not to serve as an associate minister, a "call" by the parish was not required, but he was ordained in Unity Church on December 11, 1955, with Foote and Robbins officiating.

Previously, Foote, in discussing the kind of help he needed in his parish work, had remarked that a second minister should be chosen "not as a young assistant to do whatever is left over, but to share vitally. . .in the entire ministry."[68] Notwithstanding the title of "assistant minister," Walrath did "share vitally" in the concerns of the church. Among other things he initiated an Adult Discussion Group and was instrumental in making the Lay Calling Committee into an active organization.

---

[68] Report of the Minister, annual meeting, January 1955.

Figure 33 Ronald J. Walrath, 1955-1959
Minnesota Historical Society

One particularly advantageous result of Walrath's ministry was
the institution of summer Sunday services, a benefit never
before proffered to Unity Church members. In fact, the closing
of the church in the summer months had once evoked the
remark from Wallace Robbins (as Mrs. William Dunn recalls)
that at Unity Church, "God is in his holy temple—except in
June, July, and August." The new 9:30 morning services were
conducted by Walrath for seven weeks of the summer.

The establishment of the branch church also came under the
aegis of the assistant minister. In the fall of 1955, Walrath and
Mrs. Orville Peterson met with a group of Unitarians to

organize such a branch at White Bear Lake. It was agreed that not only should the new organization have an ex-officio representative on the Board of Unity Church, but also that some financial provision would be made for it in the 1956 Unity Church budget. The White Bear Lake Branch, on its Charter Sunday, November 18 of the following year, listed thirty-five family memberships, a Sunday attendance of about thirty-seven, and a total church school enrollment of forty-five. In 1959 the branch became the North Suburban Unitarian Church and was accepted by the AUA as an independent Fellowship, releasing Unity Church from further financial responsibility. Later renamed the White Bear Unitarian Society, the Fellowship attained church status and called its first minister in 1966.

The welfare of people, also a concern of Unity Church members, led to the undertaking of two main programs. Of special importance was the work of the Displaced Persons Committee which was established in 1951 for the purpose of assisting refugees to enter this country and of providing sponsorship for them. The program was instituted when Unity Church learned that many Transylvanian Unitarians living in D.P. camps were seeking entrance into the United States to avoid being sent back to Communist Romania. Although no funds for this effort were included in the regular budget, the church did assume much of the financial responsibility by enlisting various groups and individuals to sponsor refugee families. The church members who were on this committee were Charles Sommers, Samuel H. Morgan, Mr. and Mrs. Harold Mooney, Dr. Woodard Colby, Orville Peterson, Mrs. C. C. DeCoster, Mrs. Axel von Bergen, Carl S. Miller, and L. T. Durrant.

Only a minority of those persons sponsored by the church were Unitarians, the Endre Toths and the Ambruses (already mentioned) being among this group. The Toths entered the United States under the sponsorship of the Elizabeth Eliot Club and have continued to make their home in St. Paul. The Elguther family was sponsored by four separate individuals and the Elizabeth Eliot Club. Ernst Elguther and his wife,

Christa, now also St. Paulites, have consistently played an important role in Unity Church.

The last family to be undertaken by the committee was that of Dr. Kalman Govrik, a Catholic. It also presented the most difficulties. Doctors were hard to re-establish in this country, the family was large, and Govrik had great trouble mastering the English language. When he finally obtained an internship at St. Mary's Hospital in Duluth, the church supplemented his income for several years with the contribution of one-half of the Easter offering. At length Govrik became financially independent and although of a different religion, has for some years made an annual contribution to Unity Church.

Also of interest was the work of the Neighborhood Problems Committee. The chief project of this group was the co-sponsor ship of the Park Christian Center, which was established in 1953 by the Park Baptist Church and other Baptist leaders as a means of reducing juvenile delinquency in the Summit-Hill area. Unity Church contributed to this effort by giving financial aid as well as by permitting use of space in the building for jazz band practice and other approved activities.

In 1958 the church's participation in both the Displaced Persons program and the Park Christian Center came to an end. At the same time more interest was being awakened to the needs of the people living in the poorer neighborhood of the church. The Board, working in conjunction with a Community and Social Services Project Committee, assisted in finding new housing for the four hundred families displaced by the construction of the St. Anthony Expressway. Also, representatives from the church were delegated to urge the city council to vote against new business ventures which would be disadvantageous to this area. And, in March of 1957, the church membership endorsed the proposed Open Occupancy Ordinance of the City of St. Paul.

Within the community of the church itself, the women's organizations continued their activities. The Minister's Guild, under the able leadership of its various presidents, has, on occasion, made as much as $2,300 in a year by means of bazaars, fairs, sales, and other enterprises. Of these proceeds, $500 has been an annual contribution towards the support of the minister's contingency fund, the balance being independently voted to worthwhile causes such as the Unitarian-Universalist Service Committee, the Unitarian-Universalist Women's Federation Diabetic Camp, and Meadville Theological School. Between 1968-71 the Guild raised $3,500 with the generous help of gifts from the Library Committee, the Elizabeth Eliot Club, and individual church members. The total sum was applied to a special publication fund for the printing of Arthur Foote's volume of meditations, to be released sometime in 1972.

The members of the Women's Alliance (in existence since 1897), continued to meet regularly at the church for sociability and their needlework projects. By the late sixties, however, the Alliance had dwindled in numbers and therefore voted to merge with the younger and more active Minister's Guild.

At the present time, the Elizabeth Eliot Club, functioning without professional help, still maintains its sponsorship of the Amity group founded in 1956. The fifteen members of Amity are "old-timers" who have been out of the hospital for a long time and who need each other as well as some assistance from their Elizabeth Eliot Club sponsors.

For the church school the last half of this decade brought two interesting developments. One involved the Christmas pageant and was, in part, a consequence of the changing makeup of the congregation. Whereas in previous years, the church membership had been composed largely of "birthright" Unitarians (many of them of the second or third generation), gradually Unity Church was attracting persons formerly of more orthodox faiths, and the "old-time" Unitarians were no longer in such preponderance. The newer members, who had rejected the Bible as gospel, regarded the pageant as totally unrelated to a liberal religion. Out of these differences a controversy arose in 1955 between the conservatives who desired to hold fast to their beloved Christmas tradition and those members who were disturbed by the drama's implied acceptance of an atypical Unitarian theological position. To work out a presentation more representative of Unitarian ideas and still incorporate much of the old, Mrs. Orville Peterson, chairman of the Pageant Committee, co-operated with Mrs. Harry Bratnober, Mrs. William Hughes, and Arthur Foote in revising the narrative. The new script called for a reading of both the Matthew and Luke versions of Jesus' birth, a device aimed at pointing up the marked differences in the two gospels and emphasizing the nonmiraculous, nonsupernatural aspects of the Christmas story. The pageant was presented in its new form for two years, and evaluated each time. But, at the annual meeting in February, 1957, it was found that the traditionalist's voice was still a strong one and the vote, by a small majority, favored a return to the original dramatization.

The other development was a happy experiment which became an immediate success. This was the opening of a church Day Camp at the home of the James E. Klingels in the summer of 1957. The session was one week long and during the first year included only fourth and fifth graders. The reception of this venture was so enthusiastic that the Day Camp soon became a firmly established part of the church school program, involving more classes, teen-age assistants, parents, and teachers. This program was terminated after the summer of 1971.

The 1950's offered numerous occasions for celebrations of anniversaries and commendations for length of service in the church. In 1953 Mrs. Powell completed twenty-five years of outstanding work both as organist and director of the choir; James Klingel began the first year of his (to date) seventeen year term as treasurer of the church; John Schlenck, Sr., had already served thirteen of his total seventeen years as chairman of the Ushering Committee. In 1957 this post was assumed by William R. Anderson, Jr., who continues in it today. Brock Reynolds came to work as church custodian in 1955 and remained until his death in 1969. In years of service to the church, Emma Evenoskis had one of the longest records. She began her job of housekeeping at the church in the early thirties, not retiring until 1961, near the end of her life. And these are only a few of the many who have contributed long and loyally to the support of Unity Church.

Another highlight of this decade was the church's eightieth anniversary in 1952, and naturally, the occasion called for a party. The program for the evening was entitled "A Short History of Unity Church with a Light Musical Touch." It consisted of a series of tableaux featuring bridal couples and an officiating minister, all suitably costumed in the fashions of the times of Gannett (1870), Crothers (1890), Eliot (1920), and Foote (1950). Some of the wedding gowns were loaned by the Minnesota Historical Society and others were borrowed from church members. Mrs. James Holman, dressed in her grandmother's gown, represented the 1870's; Edgar Ober, as Crothers, officiated for Miss Anne Steele and Dr. Harry Ogden, the happy couple of the 1890's; and Mrs. Wesley Madsen modeled the 1920 version worn by Mrs. James Holman at her own wedding. With Louis Headley as master of ceremonies; Wesley Madsen at the piano, rendering popular music of each period portrayed; a script by Mrs. Charles Park; publicity in the hands of Mrs. William West, Jr.; with the program directed by Miss Sarah Converse, and with Frederick Eliot present as the speaker of the evening, the affair could not fail to be an overwhelming success.

Another propitious time for celebrating occurred three years later, on May 10, 1955, on the tenth anniversary of Foote's ministry in St. Paul. The presence of the minister's parents provided a particularly happy note to the occasion.

This event, sponsored by the Minister's Guild, was under the direction of Mrs. Watson P. Davidson, Jr. A verse composed by Mrs. William West, Jr., requested one dollar from every interested member for a cash gift for the Footes. Dinner was prepared and served by the Elizabeth Eliot Club.

The highlight of the evening was an original skit by William F. Davidson entitled "The Unfinished Sermon." In it the audience observed the minister, played by Hamilton Ross, surrounded by all the paraphernalia of church groups, such as packing boxes for Korea, apples for sale, and choir robes. He struggles to write his sermon through endless interruptions, including a visit from the janitor, fretting that the coal bin is empty; Sarah Converse, leaning over "Foote's" shoulder to correct his spelling; a choir member who deposits a large dog for the minister to tend; a union leader who informs "Foote" that his singing with the congregation is against union rules. The last arrival is the minister's wife, holding a baby in her arms. After informing her husband that she is on the way to a meeting of a Committee to Lighten the Minister's Load, she de– parts, leaving the baby in the minister's lap.

The performance ended with the choir singing "I Am a Unitarian," (a parody on the Major-General's ditty in *The Pirates of Penzance* by Gilbert and Sullivan) and some nonsense verses pertaining to Arthur Foote's talents and hobbies. The song and three verses of the poem follow.

> I am the very pattern of a modern Unitarian,
> I used to be a Catholic or p'rhaps a Presbyterian.
> I know the Bible stories, and I quote the Upanishad,
> The wisdom of Confucius, and Shintoism, too, by gad.
> I'm also well acquainted with Count Tolstoy and with Socrates,
> With Channing and Ralph Emerson; I never make a mock of these.
> For tolerance of others' views I have a very special flair
> Unless they are opposed to mine, that is to say, quite doctrinaire.
> I try to serve my fellow man, in order to improve his lot,
> Using my best casseroles and keeping full my coffee pot.
>
> CHORUS
> In short in matters civic and, of course, humanitarian
> I am the very model of a modern Unitarian.
>
> This clerical fellow can paint,
> But he sighs with a mild complaint,
> "If my time were not so
> I might be a Van Gogh.

But that's one thing I maybe just ain't."

A sail can be quite a thriller
With Admiral Foote at the tiller;
As you watch him out there,
Praise the power of prayer
Without which he'd probably spill 'er.

Our minister's badgered and harried;
His talents are many and varied;
Well may you ask
With a tentative gasp
When DID he find time to get married?

In 1958, Elizabeth Whitman herself was honored at a church dinner given in appreciation of her ten years of excellent direction of the Sunday school, years in which the classes had developed so tremendously not only in size but in concepts and scope.

Certainly this period had been one of transition, embracing a new building, a new congregation, the addition of a second minister, and above all growth in numbers and composition of the parish. But most importantly, Unity Church had demonstrated that, as Wallace Robbins once said, "In our honest differences we work together."

VIII. "A New Commencement" 1960-1972

The 1960's presented a number of stimulating challenges to Unity Church. It was a time of changing ideas and a changing congregation, and of growing awareness of the problems in the neighboring community. The minister's responsibilities had be–come even greater. The parishioners faced a controversy over the proposed uses of a large bequest, a disastrous fire in the church, and the retirement of their minister of twenty-five years.

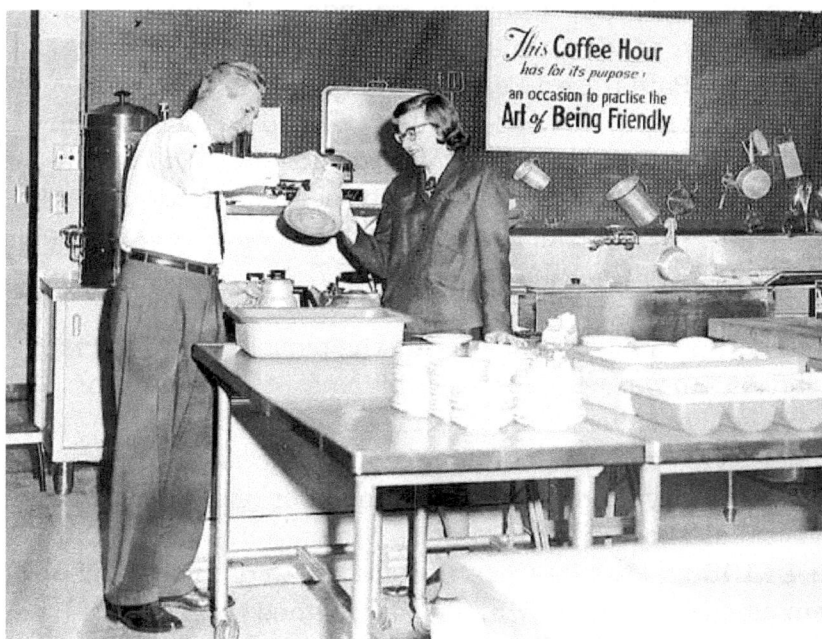

Figure 34 Coffee hour at Unity Church, appr. 1960
Minnesota Historical Society

But in the early years of this decade the tremendous growth in membership (a characteristic of Unitarianism all over the country) began to subside at Unity Church. And by the middle of the sixties the Sunday school enrollment started to decline. Still, the statistics of this period indicate that the needs of the parish called for further increases in financial support, in salaries, in committees, and in programs. The proposed budget for 1960-61 rose to just over $68,000, of which $9,900 was allocated for the minister's salary, and $5,200 for the salary of the director of religious education. The total Sunday attendance, including the church school, averaged six hundred persons.

Aside from the parish responsibilities, there were other demands upon the minister's time. Foote had already held numerous positions in outside organizations, including the following: president of the St. Paul Council of Human Relations; vice– president of the Minnesota Welfare Conference, 1957-58; chairman, Friends of Chamber Music; board member of the Minnesota Council on Religion and Race, the St. Paul Urban League, and the National Association for the Advancement of Colored People, as well as chairman of the Citizens' Committee for Open Occupancy, 1958-59. Within the denomination he served simultaneously on the boards of the American Unitarian Association and the Western Unitarian Conference, 1954-57.

Foote's active involvement outside the parish continued into the sixties. He was, at this time, chairman of the board of Meadville Theological School (and is currently a board member), vice-chairman of Governor Andersen's Mental Health Advisory Committee, and a member of the Unitarian-Universalist Association's Commission on Religion and the Arts. In 1956 he had been named chairman of the Hymnbook Commission of the UUA, which was assigned the task of revising and editing a new hymnal. This difficult, but to Foote, exciting job culminated in *Hymns for the Celebration of Life* and constituted a major contribution to the Unitarian denomination. The book, published in 1964, combined the old and the new, using many original and unfamiliar sources for both words and music. In Foote's estimation the work of the committee would be an important influence in the liberal religious movement and had also broadened the scope of his own ministry.

It was evident that Foote needed some relief and more time for study and writing. This became particularly acute when the assistant minister, Ronald Walrath, resigned in 1959. To handle some of the detail work the Board engaged Mrs. Lucy Potter as administrative assistant. She assumed this position, on a part time basis, in January of 1960. Guest speakers permitted Foote an occasional respite from the Sunday sermon. Somewhat later, the office personnel was augmented by two secretaries, Mrs. Gertrude Hatch, who also joined the staff in 1960, is still at Unity Church Mrs. Hazel Nelson began work in 1961 and remained for nearly ten years.

Probably of little assistance to Foote, but of value in other ways, was the ministerial internship program instituted at this time. At the request of the Meadville school, Unity Church agreed to assist in this training by accepting a fourth-year student as an intern for a ten-to-twelve-month period. The young man who came from Meadville in September of 1961 was Kenneth N. Helms. He received no salary during this time, but was provided with housing and reimbursed for other expenses, the larger portion of which was supplied, in this instance, by the Minister's Guild.

Helms shared in the activities of the Sunday school and the Tower Club, and among other duties, delivered an occasional ser mon. The intern's presence in St. Paul during the summer months once again made Sunday services available to the congregation, at least through July, and, at the intern's discretion, through August. In fact, Helms was only the first of a series of Meadville students to receive this kind of training at Unity Church and to contribute, each in his own way, to the life of the parish. The expenses incurred by the interns succeeding Helms were included in the regular budget. The names of the students, their periods of internship, and their current pastorates are listed here.

1960-61	Kenneth N. Helms	Unitarian Fellowship of Redwood City, California.
1961-62	Paul H. Beattie	All Souls Unitarian Church, Indianapolis, Indiana.
1962-63	Neil H. Shadle	Faculty Fellow Center for Urban Ministry, Meadville Theological School, Chicago, Illinois.
1963-64	Minister's sabbatical year, no intern.	
1964-65	Michael D. O'Kelly	First Unitarian Church, Muncie, Indiana.
1965-66	Wyman A. Rousseau, Jr.	First Congregational Unitarian Society, Westboro, Massachusetts.

At the approach of Unity Church's ninetieth anniversary Foote appealed to his parishioners (annual meeting, 1961) not to allow the church to become rigid, but to maintain its tradition of open-mindedness towards new, even revolutionary, ideas and ways. A roster of activities of this period discloses a variety of experiments, many of which, although perhaps not "revolutionary," gave emphasis to two goals in line with Arthur Foote's concept of the church's role; those of enriching the common life of the congregation and of offering opportunities of true fellowship as a means of solving the problems of an urban and changing membership. A number of these ventures resulted from ideas put forth by the Growth and Development Division, one of the units formed in a general regrouping of all the church committees.

An Art Committee, established in 1960, began its presentations of amateur and professional works. Several members of the church, including the minister, were among the exhibitors in the Center Room of the Eliot Wing. Musical events became more frequent; drama and adult discussion groups developed. To encourage a friendlier atmosphere among the membership, laymen's luncheons, family nights, and neighborhood meetings were added to the church schedule. The Growth and Development Division even promoted an enthusiastic fling at printing a parish newspaper, "The St. Paul Unitarian." Unfortunately, this publication was short-lived, despite the competence of its editors, Mrs. R. K. Patterson, Irving Lipove, and Timothy Blodgett.

Some innovations were introduced on Sunday mornings. The two sessions of the Sunday school were augmented by expanded classes held from 9:30 to 12:15, offering the students direct experience in the natural and physical sciences as well as creative work in art and dramatics. The first year's experiment with one class was so successful that gradually more classes became involved. A morning nursery, providing care for one to three-year-olds, was tried tentatively under the direction of Mrs. Robert Greenman, assisted by high school students. And, following a suggestion made by Foote some years before, the traditional practice of passing collection plates in church was abolished, to permit the spiritual mood of the Sunday service to be sustained without the intrusion of more worldly matters.

As Arthur Foote's St. Paul ministry neared its eighteenth year, it was generally agreed that the parish owed its minister a leave of absence as a token of its appreciation. In 1961 plans were already underway for a sabbatical year to take place in 1963-64, and arrangements concerning an interim minister were discussed.

In June of this same year, Foote announced that Unity Church had been named the beneficiary of a $100,000 bequest from Mrs. Donald Culver. This was the largest single contribution ever to be received by the church to date, and, ironically, the fact that the donor had given it "with no strings attached," caused a good deal of dissension within the membership. Partially as a result of this bequest (the establishment of an agency to handle gifts of this nature had already been considered), the Growth and Development Committee thought it advisable to set up a separate foundation to receive the Culver money and any other substantial amounts presented to Unity Church. Such a foundation would enable those who wished to contribute to the wider field of Unitarianism to do so locally rather than through regional or national organizations. It was the consensus of the committees involved that the Culver funds should be used in this manner, and not specifically for Unity Church or for an endowment to relieve the membership of its normal financial obligations. Accordingly, initial plans for the Channing Foundation of Minnesota were drafted by Perry M. Wilson, Jr., Samuel Morgan, Louis Headley, and James Klingel. It incorporated at the end of June 1961, under the Minnesota Non-Profit Corporation Act.

The membership was more fully informed about the Culver gift, the Channing Foundation, and the Growth and Development Division's recommendations as to possible uses for the bequest in a panel discussion presented at the October annual meeting. Not unexpectedly, opposing Unitarian reactions were immediate and definite. Opinion split between those who favored spending the money on the "bricks and mortar" of the church and those who concurred with the committees' proposal for a foundation. Backing the views of the former group was Philip W. Fitzpatrick, who, as a close friend of Mrs. Culver, felt he was cognizant of her unspoken wishes in this matter. He expressed the firm conviction that the donor intended that her gift be used specifically for the direct benefit of Unity Church, not for broader denominational purposes.

The Unitarians also diverged sharply on the question of management of the fund; whether it should be administered by the Channing Foundation, as suggested by the Growth and Development Division, or by the Board of Trustees. There were several objections to the latter plan; reliance on an endowment could weaken the willingness of the church members to assume financial responsibilities; the Board lacked both the time and the continuity in membership to administer a fund; a reserve fund for emergency use already existed.

Failure to reconcile the differences necessitated a postponement of any decisions until further discussions could be held. Small group meetings were then scheduled to allow every member the opportunity of becoming informed and of expressing a viewpoint. So it was not until the annual meeting of 1962, after the committee had compiled the material resulting from these discussions, that a second confrontation occurred. Again Unitarian minds did not meet.

The decision finally arrived at that evening was a compromise, made possible by Charles Lesley Ames's amendment to the resolution of the Growth and Development Division, and by a motion offered by Samuel Morgan, as an appeasement to the "bricks and mortar" contingent. The amendment included these modifications; the $100,000 was to be retained by Unity Church as a special fund in a special account of the First Trust Company, the investment of the funds to be the responsibility of the church's Investment Committee, with the advice of the designated Trust Company officer; neither income nor principal could be applied to the ordinary expenses of the church, with the exception of $25,000 to be set aside for sanctuary improvement (Morgan's motion); but the income from the fund could be spent on the church for special purposes; income or principal could, by special action of an annual meeting, be used for permanent improvements to the church.

Administration of the Culver fund was assigned to the newly formed Distribution Committee, composed of four members of the Investment Committee and five more members of the church chosen by the Board, including the church treasurer, ex-officio. The Channing Foundation set up its own board of from three to seven directors, the majority of whom had to be Unitarians. It was activated in 1965 and pursued its original plan of assisting broader denominational and related programs. The ever-present question of what to do with the sanctuary windows was resolved at last. Final plans for this project were in the last stages of completion; the summer of 1963 had been specified as the time for replacing the windows as well as for refurbishing the chancel; the Church Window Subcommittee had been dignified with the name of the Sanctuary Improvement Committee, and $25,000 was now within that committee's grasp.

But on February 12, 1963, fire broke out in the church. It spread rapidly from the organ loft, where it had started, to the chancel and through the sanctuary, gutting it. Smoke filled the parish hall and the Ames Chapel. But the Eliot Wing, separated from the rest of the church by heavy doors, escaped damage. Fortunately, no one was injured.

There was to have been a meeting of the Archives Committee that day, and Elwood Maunder, archives chairman, was already at the church, as were Brock Reynolds and some members of the staff. The minister was attending a laymen's luncheon but returned hastily when informed by Elizabeth Whitman of the fire. Maunder was responsible for having previously gathered much of the church's historical material from various dusty corners of the building, and now, in company with several others, retrieved these and additional church records from the wet and smoky basement room where they were filed. Naturally, destruction of the sanctuary which held so many cherished memories was an emotional shock to all concerned, particularly to those who were on the scene at the moment. Maunder has commented on the admirable control displayed by Arthur Foote in the face of this loss. In fact, after the first effects of the catastrophe subsided, the minister is said to have mustered a show of humor by remarking (though the story may be apochryphal), "Well, that takes care of the sanctuary windows."

Almost immediately generous help came from many quarters. Churches, synagogues, and other institutions in the area offered the use of space in which the Unitarians might hold Sunday services. Hymnbooks were collected and sent from Unitarian churches in other cities. Some financial donations were received. It was soon found that a few basement rooms could be readied within a week to allow the first through third grades to resume classes, and those in the Eliot Wing could continue as before. Still others were accommodated at the Selby Community Center, which, situated diagonally across the street from Unity Church, was selected as the most convenient place to conduct Sunday services, also.

The calamity of the fire again brought up some serious thoughts on the alternative of erecting a new structure at a new location instead of repairing the damage to the old church. The determining reasons for remaining at the present site were similar to those considered before, in the 1950's, at the time of the addition of the Eliot Wing; the location was accessible to a majority of the membership, and it offered an opportunity to help the surrounding low-income area by its presence in the neighborhood.

Arthur Foote was urged to proceed with his sabbatical leave in spite of the fire. Consequently, he and Mrs. Foote left St. Paul on July 1, to spend the summer in Maine before embarking on a tour of the Mediterranean. Meanwhile, an invitation had been extended to Lon Ray Call to serve as interim minister in Foote's absence.

Call is a native of North Carolina and has been in the Unitarian ministry since 1923. He has served pastorates at the First Unitarian Church of Louisville, Kentucky, All Souls Church, Braintree, Massachusetts, and the South Nassau Unitarian Church, Freeport, New York, which he founded in 1950, and of which he is minister emeritus. Much of his career has been spent in Unitarian administrative work, as executive secretary of the Western Unitarian Conference and minister-at-large of the American Unitarian Association. During these years he founded thirteen churches, and created the plan for Unitarian Fellowships. Following his retirement in 1960 and a two-and-a-half-year trip around the world with his wife, Lucy, Call served as interim minister for a ten-month period at the Thomas Jefferson Memorial Unitarian Church in Charlottesville, Virginia. He has lived in Seattle, Washington, since leaving St. Paul.

Figure 35 Lon Ray Call
Minister of Unity Church, 1963-1964
Minnesota Historical Society

The church's situation was certainly not the most favorable one
for the commencement of a new ministry. But in his short
interval in St. Paul Call won the respect and affection of the
congregation.

Even the hard, noisy chairs and the choir's inadequate seating
arrangements in the bare auditorium of the Center did not
deter the Sunday churchgoers. Despite the disruption caused

by the fire, the church appeared to run smoothly. The Sunday school, even with curtailed classes, enrolled an additional fifty children, which, as Elizabeth Whitman remarked, was, under the circumstances, a mixed blessing. Much of the credit for the year's success must go to the staff and the Board of Trustees, all of whom put in innumerable extra hours to accomplish this, as well as to the many other parishioners who generously gave their services wherever and whenever needed.

As soon as possible the Board of Trustees appointed a Building Committee, selecting Norris Jackson as chairman, and Bartlett Baker as co-chairman. The committeemen were Hamilton Ross, Harry Bratnober, Ernst Elguther, Lindsay Power, and Mrs. Harry Barnes. The firm of Hammel and Green was again commissioned to draft the architectural plans, and the building contract was awarded to Whitney Boardman's firm, Shelgren and Company.

By November 13, 1963, reconstruction was underway, with the anticipated date of completion set for one year later. The stone walls being intact, the exterior of the church remained as it was originally. The interior of the sanctuary was essentially unchanged in shape and style of construction. It was found that the red cedar beams were merely scorched and a majority of the oak pews could also be salvaged. But Hammel's design substituted brightness, spaciousness, and modern simplicity for the former rather sombre dignity typical of the early 1900's. The plastered walls were painted a light color to contrast with dark-stained trusses and pews. Two new features were a skylight, casting sunlight over the chancel, and a reredos of light wood (designed by Richard Hammel) reaching from the floor to the roof peak in undulating vertical waves of graduated sizes.

Another innovation was the placing of a balcony at the rear of the sanctuary to house the organ and the choir and to insure improved acoustics. The new arrangement furnished limited space, however, and dictated the need for a smaller organ. The Music Committee, after a thorough search, found that just such an instrument, a tracker organ, was obtainable from the

Figure 36 Rear of the sanctuary showing the Noack organ
Photograph by Eugene D. Becker

company of Fritz Noack of Lawrence, Massachusetts. More than a year was required to build and install the organ at a cost of $55,000.

In the parish hall the old stage was removed to provide more space, and a new entrance from the sanctuary to the parish hall afforded better access to and from both rooms. Much needed office space for the music director, the ministerial intern, and the administrative assistant was also made available. Practical rearrangements in the basement increased classroom space and improved traffic flow.

A totally new addition, a cloister, was included in the final building plans. This caused dismay on the part of some members because of its orthodox connotations, objections from others because of the added expense involved, and much general discussion as to what this new feature should be called. It was built primarily to overcome traffic bottlenecks and to offer space where members could visit and hang their coats. The cloister also benefited the church by providing a street level entrance on Portland Avenue and an attractive enclosed courtyard.

Insurance on the church building had foresightedly been raised to $562,000 a few years before the fire. This enabled the insurance adjustor to obtain a final settlement of $281,690 (exclusive of his fee). A rebuilding campaign was launched immediately and the response from the membership was gratifying. By April of 1965 pledges had brought in more than $65,000. The church was able to finance the remaining cost of construction by means of $12,000 from interest on investments, nearly $10,000 from bequests, and $50,000 taken from the Culver fund. One-half of the latter amount was the sum allocated for sanctuary improvement when the Culver fund was set up in 1962. The additional $25,000 was voted, in accordance with the amendment, at a special parish meeting in 1964, and was approximately the amount necessary for the inclusion of the cloister. Of the bequest money, $5,000 was a gift from the Misses Laura and Anita Furness, and enabled the church to include some extra items not otherwise feasible. The total cost of the rebuilding came to $441,000. It was entirely paid up by December of 1967.

Almost all of the work, exclusive of the installation of the organ, was completed by the time Foote returned to resume his ministry. In his first sermon in the rebuilt church (September 13, 1964) Foote spoke of the sanctuary's new spaciousness and heightened sense of the vertical, which made it a more inviting place to worship. And at the annual meeting shortly thereafter, he expressed his own and the congregation's appreciation for the interim minister's services during a difficult time. Call had generously set aside the $500 allotted for occasional substitutes in the pulpit, requesting that the money be used for new hymnals for the church. Foote said further that he found the congregation stronger and more closely knit, proving that its "fundamental loyalties are placed not in a person but in

Figure 37 The sanctuary as it looks today

moral, spiritual, and social values this church exists to
support."

In recognition of those who worked on the rebuilding
project, the architect, the contractor, the craftsmen, and
the workmen, and as a means of thanking them for their
interest and skill in the enterprise, Unity Church invited
them to a special service on the Sunday before
Thanksgiving. On January 17, 1965, after the organ had
been installed, the "new" church was dedicated. A special
Sunday service was followed in the afternoon by an organ
recital, played by Henrich Fleisher, of the University of
Minnesota.

Once again, this time with the retirement of Mrs. Potter in
1965, the question of the minister's overcrowded schedule
came under scrutiny. The consensus was that Foote could
best be served by the addition to the church staff of an
associate minister. After the usual careful search, Lindsay
Power's Committee to Recommend a Minister presented a
candidate for the congregation's approval. The proposal

that the second ministerial salary be paid out of the Culver fund was also accepted by the membership. Accordingly, $30,000 from the Culver fund was applied to the annual budget, $10,000 of which would be used for the first year's total salary. Each succeeding year the amount would be decreased by $2,000 until 1970-71, the difference during these years to be made up from the annual budget.

Frederick A. Rutledge, called to Unity Church as the associate minister, is a Texan, born in San Antonio in 1931. He graduated from his home state university in 1953, and following a stint in the United States Naval Reserve, saw active duty from 1953-55. Rutledge then resumed his education, obtaining a degree of Bachelor of Divinity in 1958 from Starr King School for the Ministry at Berkeley, California. He was ordained at his first parish in Petersham, Massachusetts, where he remained for two years. Just prior to coming to St. Paul he served a four-year ministry at Danvers, Massachusetts, consolidated with the Peabody (Massachusetts) church in 1965.

The new minister made substantial contributions to Unity Church and shared fully in all parish functions, including the conducting of summer services. One of his particular interests was working with young adults. But of major concern to him were the underprivileged citizens of the city. Rutledge's efforts in their behalf were able and effective, and he became active in many organizations relating to their problems. He served on the Board of Family Service of St. Paul, and on committees of the Twin City Industrial Opportunity Committee (a job training project for the disadvantaged, originally a part of the Poverty Program, and later sponsored by ministers and laymen from various churches), the Minnesota Commission for the Legal Termination of Pregnancy, the Clergymen's Council of the Summit-University Area, and Housing Opportunities, Inc. Within the denomination

Figure 38 Frederick A. Rutledge
Minister of Unity Church, 1966-1970
Minnesota Historical Society

Rutledge worked with the Prairie Star District of the
Unitarian-Universalist Ministers (the result of a
regrouping of Midwestern states formed when the Mid-
West Conference became too large).

The last half of this decade was a time of self-searching on
the part of Unity Church. There was a feeling of
dissatisfaction with its action in the community and doubt
as to whether it was answering the needs of its large and
diversified membership. Attempts to remedy these
deficiencies, and to reach out more effectively into the
community, led to the formation of several new programs.

The Social Action Committee, open to all members of the
church, was formed in 1964 for the purpose of stimulating

the members to become acquainted with social problems and to encourage them to act on their convictions. It was the committee's job also to keep the congregation informed of specifically recommended action to be undertaken. Among other projects suggested by the committee and carried out by the church were the granting of the use of space for a tutorial program sponsored by the Urban League; membership in the Summit-University Federation (a program concerned primarily with redevelopment planning in the area); giving support and financial aid to the Loft (a teen-age recreational center), and contributing to a Leisure Age Center.

In 1968 Unity Church agreed to house a Day Care Center for three-to-five-year-olds. This program, under the jurisdiction of the Office of Economic Opportunity, was originally sponsored by the North Central Voters' League. It was permitted the use of five basement classrooms and the kitchen five days a week. The church received rent for the space but was under no obligation other than the allotting of the rooms. Currently, the Day Care Center is still in progress at the church.

Probably the most effectual undertaking in this period was that of Housing Opportunities, Inc. The prime mover of this project was Martin H. Imm, who felt that constructive and positive results in community relationship could be achieved by assisting families in the lower income area to purchase houses. The enterprise was ably and enthusiastically supported by Fred Rutledge. Imm set up a nonprofit corporation (with his wife and Morton S. Katz as co-directors) to provide mortgage financing for such home ownership by acquiring and reselling property. He enlisted the help of the Urban League Housing Office and the Housing Authority in finding buyers. The houses were owned by the corporation under a lease-purchase contract until such time as the buyer could repay in rent. A $3,000 loan from Unity Church and contributions of nearly the same amount from individuals got the program underway, and by 1970 nineteen families had purchased houses, fifteen more were in process, and another twenty-eight were waiting for the assignment of an agent. Five similar organizations have since been initiated in other churches. Arthur Foote has particularly noted that the persons responsible for this project effectively demonstrated the meaning of "the broader ministry."

Still another kind of contribution was made by the Ernst Elguthers and the A. Whittier Days, who opened their homes to two African boys. Trywell Nyirongo and Isaac Otieno came to the United States through a program sponsored by the Unitarian Service Committee to attend high school and college in this country. Unity Church shared to some extent in the financial support of the young men, whose goals were to become medical doctors.

The relationship of the church to its congregation was the concern of the Vanguard Committee. This comprised fifteen persons selected to interview a number of adult members and friends of the church as well as college-age groups to determine what the church meant to its parishioners, where its deficiencies and strengths lay, and to redefine its goals.

The younger group of Unitarians was also affected by new trends. As growth in church membership stabilized, enrollment in the church school declined. In 1970 the Sunday school enrollment dropped to a low of two hundred and fifty from the four hundred and fifty of five years earlier. One possible factor in this decrease was the smaller modern family, another may have been the popularity of family recreational weekends. In any case the slackening of interest in church school appeared to be a general pattern in churches throughout the country during this period. On the other hand, the expanded sessions continued to be successful and the attendance remained high. An interesting development was the request of the young people of Tower Club that the church membership age be lowered from eighteen to fifteen years. Their petition was granted, with the understanding that a minor must make a financial contribution separate from that of his parents to be eligible to vote.

In these years donations and memorials brought a number of welcome additions to the church. Redecoration of the Ames Chapel had been planned according to the designs of Richard Hammel, and was paid for with gifts from Mrs. Herman Kesting and Miss Perrie Jones. The purchase of a new Reuter organ to replace the old one given by the Sommers family was included in the plan, and was made possible by a gift of $5,000 from Mrs. Shedd Blodgett, a memorial to her son, Jeffrey, who was killed in World War II, and by gifts from other members. New benches for the courtyard were donated as memorials to Mr. and Mrs. Louis Hauser. A Sabathil harpsichord, given in memory of William R. Anderson, Sr., was the gift of Mrs. Anderson and William R. Anderson, Jr. Arthur Foote presented the church with a seventeenth-century English oak bench and a chair of a similar style that is a reproduction. Both pieces were Foote family heirlooms and have been placed at the rear of the sanctuary.

In 1968 the courtyard was enhanced by the addition of a piece of sculpture, created by Mrs. Gail Kristensen, a member of Unity Church. The fountain, composed of ceramic blocks of varying sizes, is the largest one of its kind in the world. The names of those whose contributions enabled the church to commission this work are listed on a plaque in the courtyard.

One supplementary acquisition was made when, in 1969, an opportunity arose to purchase the house and property to the west of the church on Holly Avenue. Approval of the purchase was voted at a special parish meeting. After some debate as to possible uses of the house, the membership agreed to a proposal made by Martin Imm by which John Baymiller, an architect, and his wife were accepted as renter-occupants for two years. Rehabilitation of the house would be done by the renter and taxes paid in lieu of rent. The advantages of this plan were that no cost devolved upon the church, the property value would be increased, the neighborhood would be benefited, and the church could take time to further investigate its ultimate use.

The close of the decade also brought to a conclusion Arthur Foote's twenty-five-year ministry. The announcement to the Board of Trustees towards the end of January, 1970, was not wholly unexpected. In a letter to the congregation, written at the same time (January 20, 1970), Foote offered his parishioners this explanation:

> The reasons for this decision are almost entirely personal; and the decision has been a long time in the making. I need not dwell upon what so many of you mean to my wife and me personally, or what the Church means as a religious community....Yet, dear as you are to both of us, I have found a steadily growing urge to make a radical change in my way of life, to change its pace and to lessen its pressures. The need to explore unused facets of myself, to cultivate undeveloped talents, to have more adequate time for thinking and creative writing seems to become ever more compelling.

Whatever the undoubted loss to the church and its individual members, the congregation was unanimous in its sentiment that, after his long and superior ministry, Foote deserved the retirement he and his wife were so eager to enjoy. His twenty–five years in St. Paul had been characterized by immeasurable concern for others, memorably beautiful services, and scholarly, contemplative sermons. Of no less benefit to the church was Foote's sensitive aesthetic taste, whether in architecture, in poetry reading, or in music. Befittingly, on the recommendation of the Board of Trustees, Foote was elected minister emeritus of Unity Church.

The resignation was effective as of April 30, 1970. The Footes' decision was to return to their house in Southwest Harbor, Maine, where there would be time and opportunity for hobbies as well as for study and writing. Foote also planned to complete his volume of meditations, specifically requested by the Minister's Guild.

The send-off party for Arthur and Rebecca Foote was held on April 24, and had been purposefully designed to be not a "farewell," but a celebration of their years at Unity Church, and, as Foote termed it, "a new commencement."

The evening began with a dinner honoring the Footes. The parish hall was packed and guests overflowed into the Eliot Wing classrooms. The candlelit dinner was accompanied by the music of roving players (the Frank Winsor family), and climaxed with a toast to the guests of honor (the occasion warranting a slight departure from an old-age bias against use of liquor in the church).

In the sanctuary the "stage" was set for the evening's program, a multi-media affair arranged by Mrs. Don Ardell. The script, brainchild of the Ernst Elguthers, assisted by the Misses Elizabeth Whitman and Lucy Raudenbush, depicted the minister in a dilemma—that of choosing between the two women in his life, his wife and Unity Church. Look-alike stand-ins for the Footes were conveniently on hand in the persons of Mrs. John Driscoll and Hamilton Ross. The "other woman," the church, was christened "Uni" for this performance, and was personified by Mrs. Antoinette Sargent.

Scattered throughout the narration (given by Orville Peterson), were various audio-visual devices. Slides flashed back to scenes and incidents of the Footes' life, punctuating the quips about their activities and characteristics (Maine, potting, pets, beards, and the like). A chorus chanted ap propriate pronouncements in verse or prose, and, from time to time, even the choir joined in with hymns, carefully chosen to fit the text. An occasional "blub" from the organ prompted "Foote, the fixer," to make a sudden exit from the stage to attend to a persistent leak, and, as usual, the annual budget, the Board of Trustees, pledge Sunday, etc., came in for their share of the jesting.

As the program came to an end, the "real Rebecca and Arthur Foote" were summoned to the platform to receive the congregation's gift of a potting wheel, and walked out of the church under a banner that read "Welcome to Maine."

The combined efforts of many church members went into this program. In addition to those already mentioned, a few who held specific jobs are listed here.

General chairman	Mrs. Watson Davidson
Dinner	Mr. and Mrs. John Bergstedt
Table arrangements	Mrs. John Barwise
Toastmaster	Norris Jackson
Slides and artwork	John Baymiller Mrs. T. D. Wright William Bray Henry Hall Robert Shoffner
Cameramen	Mr. and Mrs. Frank Winsor the church choir
Music	Axel von Bergen Mr. and Mrs. Fred Rutledge, Miss Ruth Stryker Mrs. Warner Shippee Mrs. John Baymiller Club members
Assistants	Mrs. Watson Davidson

Fred Rutledge's contract was a co-terminal arrangement, to last only during Foote's ministry. Consequently, Foote's resignation brought to a conclusion the pastorate of the associate minister as well. By prior agreement with the church, Rutledge continued to receive his salary until he accepted another ministry. He remained at Unity Church throughout the summer of 1970, when he accepted the position of assistant minister of the First Unitarian Society in Minneapolis. In the fall of 1971 he left for Baltimore, Maryland, to serve as associate minister at the First Unitarian Church there.

Unity Church was well aware of the difficulties involved in choosing a successor to Arthur Foote. The task was complicated in this instance by the dissimilar viewpoints in the church between those who preferred a continuation of the ministerial pattern set by Foote and the group which was more willing to accept changes in church attitudes. In order to get a "profile" on what this divergent membership wanted in a new minister, the Board of Trustees published in a bulletin a request for suggestions of persons to be placed on the Committee to Recommend a New Minister (CRAM). The list was to be the committee's basis for selection. From a poll of sixty-four write-in names, the following twelve were chosen:

        T.D. Wright, Chairman
        Joesephine Downey
        James Fish
        Howard Huelster
        Mrs. Martin Imm
        Mrs. Howard Mayne
        Mrs. Orville Peterson
        Lindsay Power
        Mrs. Beatrice Reed
        Hamilton Ross
        Mrs. Warner Shippee
        Perry Wilson

Upon the request of the Tower Club, a representative from that group (Dan Huelster) was accepted as an additional committee member.

Neighborhood meetings supplied CRAM with information on the members' views in this matter and an exhaustive search for the new minister began. This involved numerous trips to other cities, many interviews, and length meetings on the part of the committee. A second hard-working group was the Pulpit Supply Committee, whose job it was to provide a speaker or a program for every Sunday until such time as the church called a minister.

The "search for excellence," carried on so thoroughly by CRAM, resulted in the candidacy of thirty-year old Roy Dennis Phillips. Following an enthusiastic vote of approval on March 1, 1971, T.D. Wright, chairman of the committee, cautioned the membership about the danger of making comparisons between a highly-successful twenty-five-year incumbent and a newcomer to the pulpit. And Foote, before leaving St. Paul, had admonished the parishioners not to be afraid of youth, reminding them that many of Unity Church's ministers, including Crothers, Eliot, Robbins, and Foote himself, had come to St. Paul as young men in their late twenties or early thirties.

Roy Phillips accepted the offer from Unity Church and arrived in St. Paul in time to deliver a few sermons before the summer vacation. He is a New Englander, born in Boston in 1941, but growing up in nearby Somerville. He began his undergraduate studies at Northeastern University in Boston, which he attended for three years, concentrating on chemical engineering. While there, Phillips became actively interested in the Student Religious Liberals, and deciding to abandon the engineering field in favor of a career in the liberal church, transferred to Boston University in 1961. Two years later, in an eventful period between spring and fall, he received his A.B. degree, married Judith Peabody, and entered Meadville Theological School. In June of 1967, he was awarded his B.D. from Meadville. The following October he was installed as minister of the Unitarian Universalist Church of Racine and Kenosha (Wisconsin.) [Now the Olympia Brown UU Church]

Phillips has had broad experience in ministerial training, in the denomination, and in community work. During his years at Meadville he served as ministerial intern to King's Chapel, Boston; as chaplain assistant at Boston State Hospital, and, in his senior year, as ministerial associate to the Benton Harbor (Michigan) Unitarian Fellowship. In addition to counseling work (Counseling Center Practicum at the University of Chicago, 1965; Conference on Aging at Pennsylvania State University, 1968), he has held positions of leadership in the denomination. He is currently president of the Central Midwest District Chapter of the Unitarian Universalist Minister's Association as well as ministerial settlement representative for the district. His many community activities include the American Civil Liberties Union, Kenosha Mental Health Association, and Wisconsin Children's Service Society.

Figure 39 The installation of Roy D. Phillips
Arthur N. Foote, minister emeritus
Photograph by Henry Hall

Judith Peabody Phillips was born in Bath, Maine, in 1943.
She met her husband when she was training to be a legal
secretary at Burdett College in Boston and has continued
this work during her marriage. The twelfth minister of Unity
Church and his wife have been officially welcomed into their
new congregational family and are occupying the familiar
parsonage at 764 Goodrich Avenue.

Unfortunately, the fall of 1971 brought to Unity Church still
another loss in valuable personnel. At the September annual

meeting the parish members were informed by Elizabeth Whitman that she had tendered her resignation, to be effective as of January 1, 1972. In her report Miss Whitman stated her reasons as the unusual length of time (twenty-three years) she had been with Unity Church and her belief that a new minister should have the option of developing a church school program in coordination with a director of religious education of his personal choice. Both congregation and minister were well aware of the debt owed to Miss Whitman, who, during the years, particularly in the absences of the ministers, had assumed responsibilities far beyond her specified work for the church school. The successive departures of Arthur Foote and Elizabeth Whitman signified the close of an era but, at the same time, the installation of an able and stimulating young minister on October 17, 1971, carried with it the expectation of a "new commencement" in the spiritual and community life of the parish.

Now Unity Church, the oldest Unitarian church in the state, is looking back over a century of existence.[69] It has had the remarkably good fortune to have been ministered to by several men of extraordinary abilities and dedication—men who have extended themselves on behalf of the parish, community, and denomination. It has been endowed with "the strength of the heritage" which is worthy of remembering.

But Unity Church, to no less a degree, is its membership. Richard Boynton said, "You, the people, have been the real Unity Church, and are so still." And it is these people, who, in looking forward as well as back, will recognize in Arthur Foote's words a challenge for the times ahead.

"The past and the present unfold into the future where our horizons are limited only by our own stature, and where our progress will be as great and as significant as we make it."

---

[69] First Universalist Church of Minneapolis is the oldest continuous UU congregation in Minnesota.

150

Updates on Unity Ministers, 2020 Edition

Wallace W. Robbins served as President of Meadville Theological Society from 1944 to 1956, and then, served as minister of First Unitarian Church in Worcester, MA from 1956 until he retired in 1975. He died of spinal cancer at home in Worcester in 1988.

After Arthur Foote II retired from Unity in 1970, he and Rebecca moved back to Southwest Harbor, Maine where he pursued pottery and published his book, *Taking Down the Defenses* (1972). He died in 1979.

After serving Unity as Assistant Minister to Arthur Foote II, Ronald J. Walrath left ministry and pursued a career at the Minnesota Historical Society History Center for many years. He died in 2019.

Frederick Rutledge went on to serve as assistant or interim minister at First Unitarian Society of Minneapolis, The First Unitarian Church of Baltimore, and the Southwest UU Church in North Royalton, Ohio before retiring in 1978.

Elizabeth "Betty" Whitman served as Unity's Director of Religious Education from 1948 until she retired in 1972. She was socially conscious, politically active, an avid reader, and enjoyed nature. She died at age 96 in 2014.

Virginia Wetherbee Powell served as Director of music ministries for 52 years. She retired in 1980, was honored with emeritus status as well as a plaque marking her contributions to Unity Church. She died at age 92 in 1995.

Roy D. Phillips served Unity Church from 1971 to 1999. After Unity, he served as interim minister in Ohio and Florida, and then accepted a call to the UU Church of Tucson in 2001. He retired in 2004 and died suddenly while visiting Morocco in 2008.

Lon Ray Call served as interim minister at Unity in his retirement years. He died in 1985.

Chairmen of the Board of Trustees of Unity Church

1872 - First Board of Trustees
    William L. Ames, Joseph S. Sewall, William H. Kelley,
    Daniel McCaine, Edward Sawyer;
    H. P. Grant, secretary and treasurer.	

1881 Joseph S. Sewall	1928,1929
1882 Edward Sawyer	Charles Lesley Ames
1883 Frederick Jackson	1930,1931,1932
1884 Edward Sawyer	Samuel E. Turner
1885 John D. Ludden	1933, 1934, 1935
1886 Daniel McCaine	Louis S. Headley
1887 John D. Estabrook	1936,1937 Julian B. Baird
1888 E. E. Woodman	1938 Harold E. Wood
1889 Judge L. W. Collins	1939,1940 E. A. Boyden
1890 John D. Estabrook	1941,1942
1891 Samuel J. Beals	Charles Lesley Ames
1892, 1893 Dr. William Davis	1943,1944,1945
1894 Charles W. Ames	Chandler B. Davis
1895 John D. Estabrook	1946 Harold E. Wood
1896 Samuel L. Sewall	1947 Harry G. Barnes
1897 John D. Estabrook	1948, 1949 1950
1898,1899 E. E. Woodman	Harry G. Huse
1900, 1901 Charles W. Ames	1951 Philip W. Fitzpatrick
1902, 1903 Francis B. Tiffany	1952 Edward M. Read
1904, 1905 E. H. Bailey	1953,1954 William L. West, Jr.
1906 Charles W. Ames	1955,1956, 1957 Irving Clark
1907 Benjamin Sommers	1958,1959 Joe A. Walters
1908 Henry E. Randall	1960 Perry M. Wilson, Jr.
1909 Francis B. Tiffany	1961 Samuel H. Morgan
1910 J. Stearns Smith	1962 Theodore D. Wright
1911 Edward B. Young	1963,1964
1912 N. M. Thygeson	Howard M. Guthman
1913, 1914 William A. Laidlaw	1965 Warren Bjorkland
1915, 1916 Edward B. Young	1966 Richard A. Marsh;
1917 Charles W. Ames	resigned; term completed
1918 Henry E. Randall	by Hyam Segell
1919, 1920 William A. Laidlaw	1967 Hyam Segell
1921 Charles L. Sommers	1968 Orville C. Peterson
1922 Edward P. Davis	1969 Roger R. Palmer
1923, 1924 Francis B. Tiffany	1970 Willard W. Fryhofer
1925,1926 Harold E. Wood	1971 Hamilton Ross
1927 G. A. Younquist	

St. Paul Locations

1852: Sons of Temperance Hall (1 service, location unknown)
1858: Hall over Pollack and Donaldson Company store,
    Robert St. bt 4th and 5th [70]
1859: Concert Hall/Philharmonic Society, Third St. bluff
1859: Good Templars Hall, 5th and Robert St.
Aug 4, 1861; May 28, 1865; July 2, 1865: Courthouse
1872: Knauft's Hall, 3rd Floor, 7th and Olive St.
1872-1875: Temperance Street church, between 8th and 9th
1875-1879: Universalist Church, Wabasha. corner 9th [71]
1879: Sherman Hall, 6th and Wabasha
1882–1905: Unity Church, East side Wabasha, opp Summit ave.[72]
1905-present: 733 Portland Ave.

Bibliography

UNITY CHURCH ARCHIVES IN THE MINNESOTA HISTORICAL
SOCIETY, ST. PAUL
    Bulletins, issued during church season.
    Church yearbooks.
    Correspondence of ministers and members.
    Crane, Edgar. How to Turn a State Upside Down, an
        undated pamphlet, possibly published in 1951.
    Manuscript histories, by William H. Kelley, Emma Kelley,
        and William Channing Gannett.
    Minutes, meetings of the Board of
    Trustees. Sermons.
    Scripts for anniversary celebrations.
INTERVIEWS AND RECOLLECTIONS OF MEMBERS OF UNITY
CHURCH
    Walter Chapin, Jr., Mary Davis, Josephine Downey,
    Arthur Foote, Mary Chapin Reisig, Martha Putnam
    Holman,
    Elizabeth Ames Jackson, Eleanor Jilson, Wallace
    Robbins, Helen James Sommers, Esther Tiffany, William
    L. West, Jr.
BOOKS AND ARTICLES
    Boynton, Richard W. "An Unspotted Soul." Unity, LVIII
        (February 7, 1907), pp. 448-51.

---

[70] St. Paul City Directory 1859
[71] St. Paul City Directory 1877
[72] St. Paul City Directory 1883

Crothers, Louise Bronson. A Family Chronicle. Concord:
    Rumford Press, 1966. (Privately printed)

Eliot, Frederick May. "A Tribute to William Channing
    Gannett." Unity, XCIII (March 6, 1924), p. 9.

Esbjornson, Robert. A Christian in Politics: Luther W.
    Youngdahl. Minneapolis: T. S. Denison & Company,
    1955.

Heralds of a Liberal Faith: The Pilots. Vol. IV. Boston:
    Beacon Press, 1952.

Malick, John. "John Dumont Reid." Christian Register,
    CVIII (June 27, 1929), p. 561.

Scott, Clinton Lee. These Live Tomorrow: Twenty Unitarian-
    Universalist Biographies. Boston: Beacon Press, 1964.

Wendte, Charles W. "Memories of William Channing Gannett."
    Unity, XCIII (March 6, 1924), pp. 4-6.

www.ingramcontent.com/pod-product-compliance
Lightning Source LLC
Chambersburg PA
CBHW081150090426
42736CB00017B/3259